Workbook

JUMP Aboard

Paul A. Davies and Amanda Cant

Contents

MACMILLAN

Time Travel!

1 Complete the pictures. Then find and write.

1 bocm

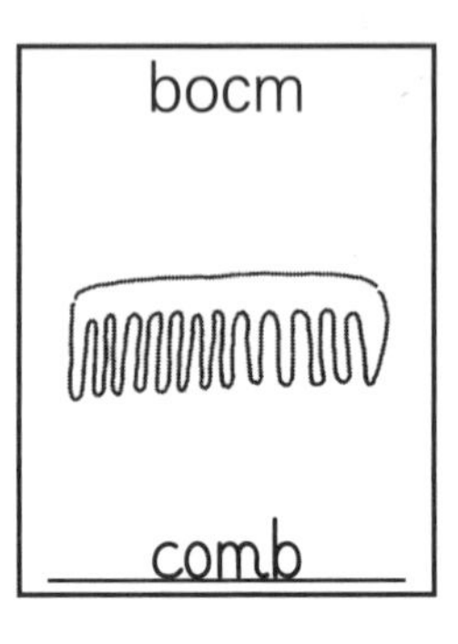

comb

2 mlpa

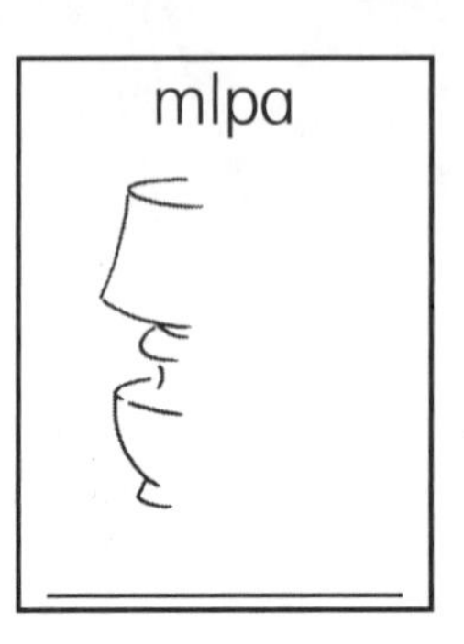

3 shces tse

4 gru

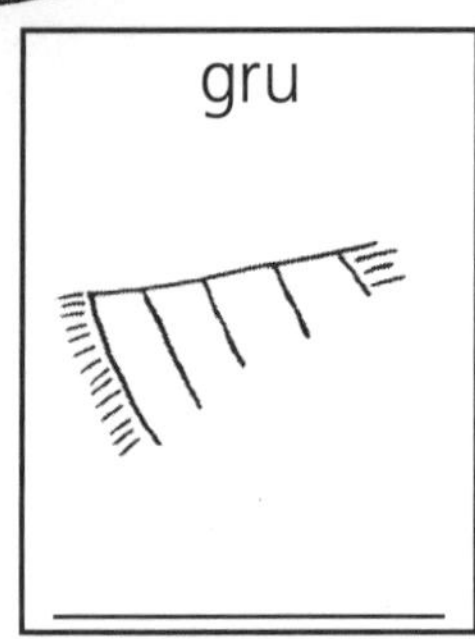

5 dlenacra

6 eosptr

7 sfacirbee

8 aramce

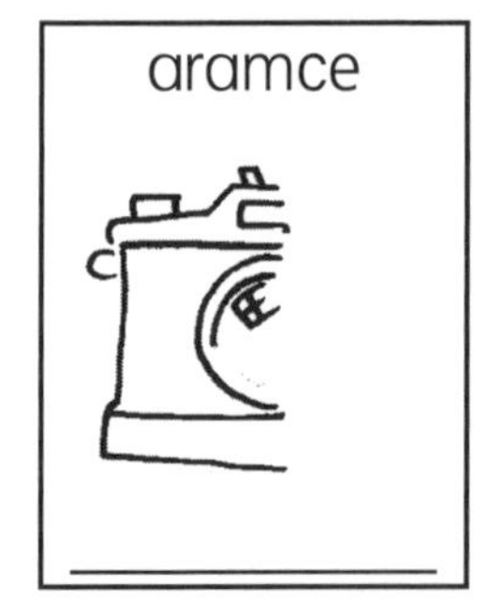

9 irmror

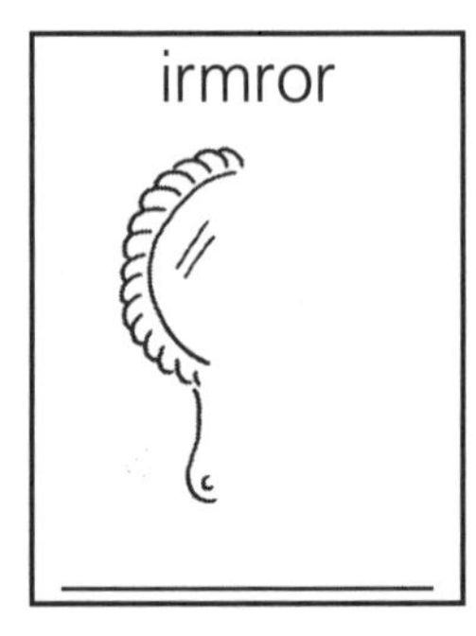

10 eobocsak

11 aptlpo

12 hsubhriar

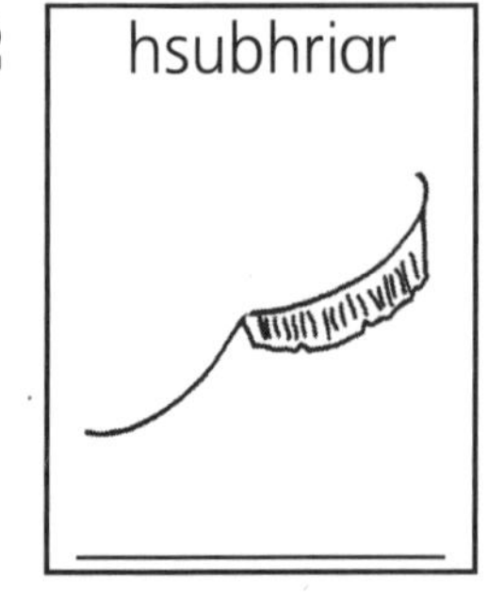

2 Look in your classroom. Then find out how many things from Activity I you can and can't see. (What about you?)

I can see ____

____.

I can't see ____

____.

1 Look and tick (✓). Then find the secret word.

		picture A		picture B	
1	He's going to listen to music.	☐	m	✓	s
2	He's going to read a book.	☐	u	☐	c
3	She's going to walk in the mountains.	☐	h	☐	s
4	He's going to swim in the sea.	☐	o	☐	e
5	She's going to watch TV.	☐	u	☐	o
6	She's going to ride a bike.	☐	l	☐	m

What are you going to do after
s _ _ _ _ _ _ ?

2 Find and write about your friends.

After school . . .

1 Who is going to read a book? Maria is going to read a book.

2 Who is going to go to a shop? ______________________

3 Who is going to listen to music? ______________________

4 Who is going to watch TV? ______________________

5 Who is going to do their homework? ______________________

6 Who is going to play on a computer? ______________________

1 Look and write *true* or *false*.

1. Cleo and Joe are going to go to the park. false
2. They are going to go to the beach. ____________
3. They are going to drink lemonade. ____________
4. They are going to play tennis. ____________
5. They are going to go to sleep. ____________

2 Answer using *Yes, I am* or *No, I'm not*.

What about you?

What are you going to do this evening?

1. Are you going to swim? ____________________
2. Are you going to send some e-mails? ____________________
3. Are you going to call your grandpa? ____________________
4. Are you going to sing 'Rock Around the Clock'? ____________________
5. Are you going to paint a picture? ____________________
6. Are you going to do your homework? ____________________

3 Write two things you are going to do and two things you aren't going to do this evening.

What about you?

This evening ____

____.

This evening ____

____.

1 Complete the puzzle.

A type of clock that's 3,500 years old. ____________	A room in your school that has a clock. ____________	A type of clock that uses sunlight. ____________	A shop that has a clock. ____________
A building that has a clock. ____________	A type of clock that needs a key. ____________	A type of clock you can use at night. ____________	A room in your house that has a clock. ____________

2 Make a sundial.

1 Draw a circle and cut it out.

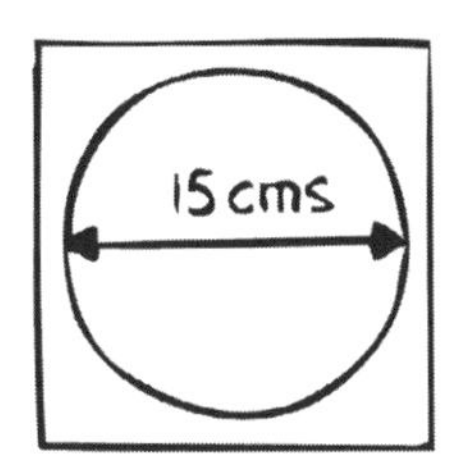

2 Push a pencil through the middle of the sundial. Put it in a sunny place.

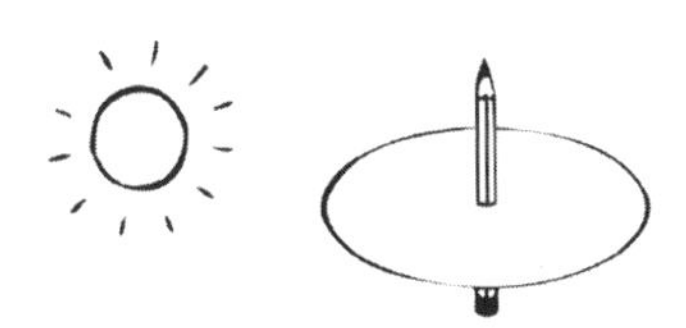

3 Find a clock. When it is 9 o'clock in the morning draw a line along the shadow. Write '9'. Do the same at 10, 11, 12 o'clock.

4 Now you can use your clock to tell the time, but don't move it!

1 Choose and write. Then match the answers.

How ~~What~~	Where	When	Who	Why

1 What are you going to drink? [d]

2 ________ are you going to go? [ ]

3 ________ are they going to get there? [ ]

4 ________ is going to take them? [ ]

5 ________ are they going to go to the beach? [ ]

6 ________ are they going to go there? [ ]

a They're going to get there by car.

b Because it's the summer holidays.

c

d

e They're going to go on Tuesday morning.

f Their dad is going to take them.

2 Match the rhyming words.

1	Where	now	not
2	Why	pen	my
3	What	hair	cow
4	How	hot	bear
5	When	fly	then

1 Complete the questions. Then write the answers.

What about you?

1 Who are you going to see this weekend?

I'm going to see Grandma and Grandpa.

2 What time ________ to get up on Saturday?

____

3 What ________ to do on Sunday afternoon?

____

4 Where ________ to go this weekend?

____

5 How many films ________ to watch this weekend?

____

2 Complete the questions. Then ask a friend and write.

Who are you going to ask? ________

1 hWat What is she / he going to watch on TV?

____

2 eWnh ________ is she / he going to go shopping?

____

3 ohW ________ is she / he going to see?

____

4 aWth ________ is she / he going to wear?

____

5 eerhW ________ is she / he going to go?

____

Phonics

1 Read.

At 11 o'**cl**ock the **cl**ass is at the **gl**ass museum.

3
How do you **cl**ean the **gl**asses?
Carefully. We wear special **gl**oves.

2 Write *cl* or *gl* to match the words in the story.

1 c l ock

2 __ __ oves

3 __ __ asses

4 __ __ ean

5 __ __ ose

3 Write *true* or *false.*

1 The class is going to visit the glass museum. ____________

2 At 10 o'clock they are at the museum. ____________

3 The glasses are beautiful. ____________

4 People clean the glasses with special shoes. ____________

Try It!

LESSON 8
UNIT 1

1 Tick (✓) the correct sentences.

1 He's going to listening to music. ☐
2 It's a digital clock. ☑
3 It need batteries. ☐
4 They're going to go to the beach. ☐
5 They're going sing a song. ☐
6 You can use an alarm clock at night. ☐
7 She's going to watch TV. ☐
8 He are sending an e-mail. ☐
9 We're going to visit the museum. ☐
10 I'm going to eat some sweets. ☐

Now correct the incorrect sentences.

1 He's going to listen to music.
2 ______
3 ______
4 ______

2 Find the verbs. Then write the questions.

1 tae eat 2 iitvs v______ 3 lmcbi c______ 4 veha h______

1 Who / What What are they going to eat ?
2 Where / When ______ is she going to ______ the museum?
3 How / What ______ are you going to ______ the mountain?
4 Who / Where ______ is he going to ______ his party?

The Challenge

1 Find the odd one out. Then write sentences.

1	listening	watch	singing	running
2	what	where	eat	when
3	do	use	visit	playing
4	laptop	see	send	paint
5	class	clock	gloves	close
6	hairbrush	go	calendar	poster

1 going to / TV I'm going to watch TV.

2 going to / breakfast ______________________

3 I like / tennis ______________________

4 I don't have / at home ______________________

5 I have / for the winter ______________________

6 going to / to the cinema ______________________

2 Find the question. Then write your answer.

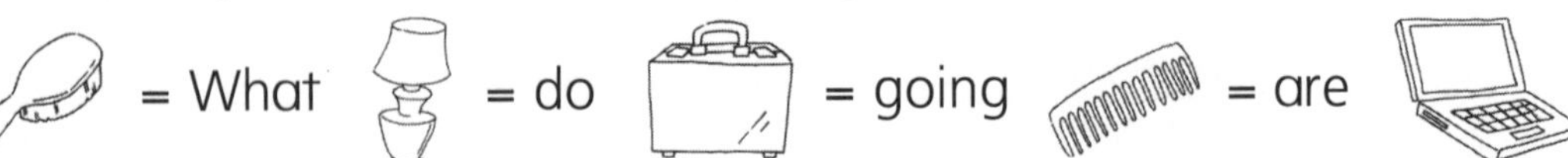
 = What  = do 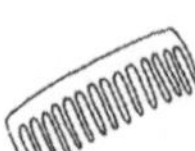 = going  = are laptop = you

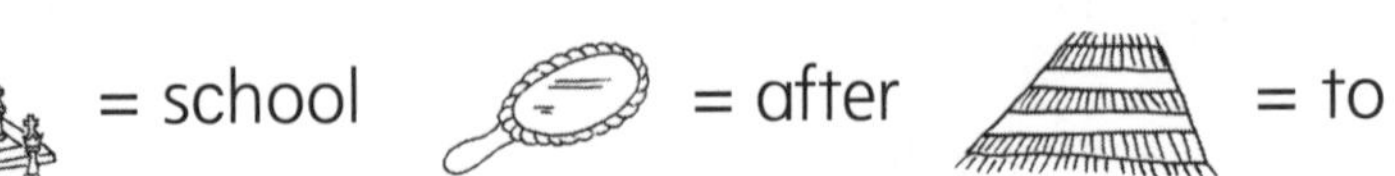
 = school 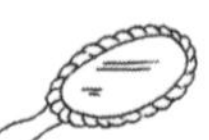 = after rug = to

hairbrush comb laptop briefcase rug lamp mirror chess set

Question: What ____ ____ ____ ____ ____ ____ ____?

Your answer: ______________________

3 Tick (✓) the words to complete Tara's message.

Collect the correct words.

1	A grandfather clock needs	batteries.	☐	An
		a key.	☑	I
2	Which word rhymes with 'who'?	two	☐	have
		now	☐	old
3	Which word rhymes with 'class'?	clock	☐	grandfather
		glass	☐	sixteen
4	Can you use a sundial at night?	yes	☐	clock
		no	☐	posters

I ________ ________ ________

How many do you have?

4 Write the labels. Then colour the picture.

Words beginning with ... c = blue b = red l = green h = yellow

Unit 2 Dinosaurs!

1 Choose.

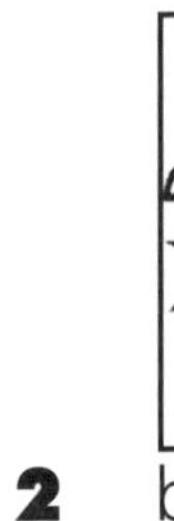
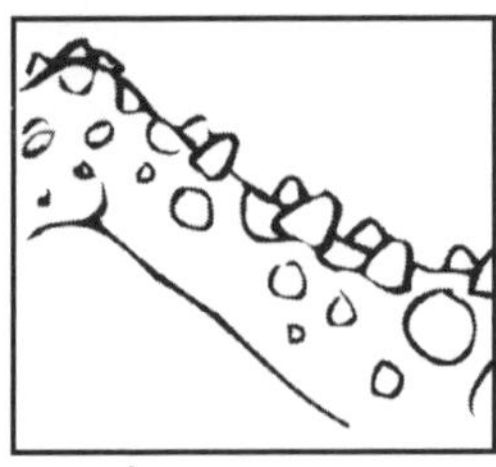
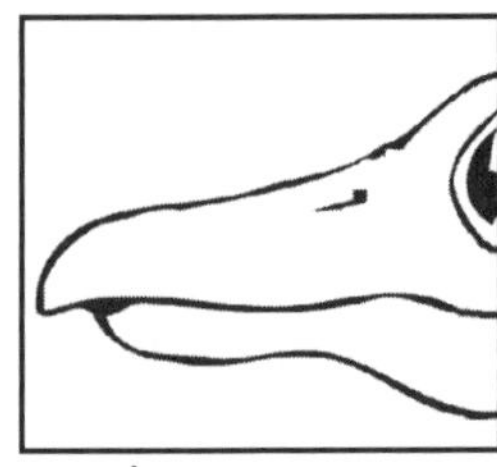

1 wings / spikes

2 beak / back

3 neck / back legs

4 scale / beak

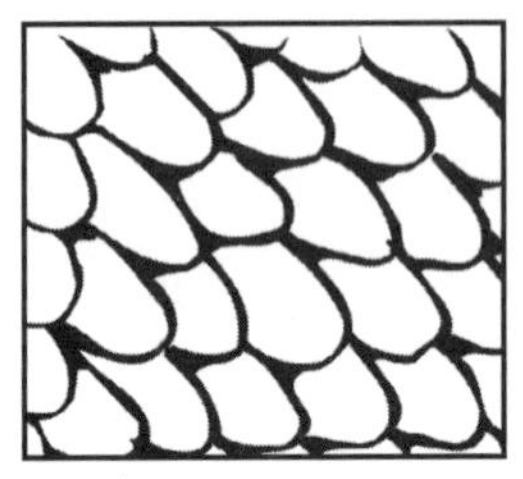

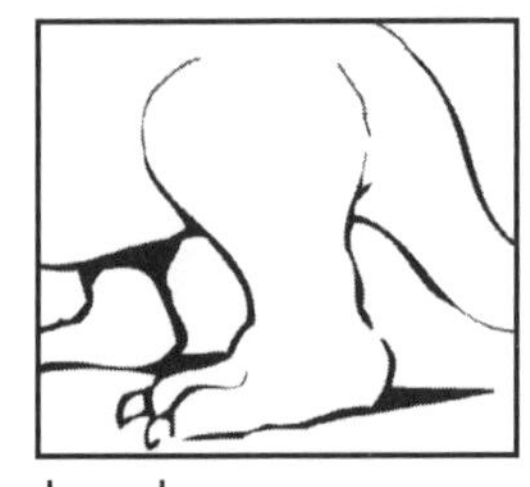

5 scales / horns

6 wing / neck

7 spikes / horns

8 back / back legs

2 Match.

1 It has horns.	kangaroo	a	
2 It has a beak.	fish	b	
3 It has scales.	giraffe	c	
4 It has a long neck.	stegosaurus	d	
5 It has strong back legs.	ostrich	e	
6 It has spikes.	triceratops	f	

1 Circle the verbs in the past tense.

asked	answer	shouted	press	changed	live
noticed	jump	turned around	turn around	jumped	notice
shout	ask	pressed	answered	lived	change

2 Look at Activity I. Then complete the chart.

Present tense	Past tense
	pressed
notice	
ask	
	changed
	jumped
shout	
live	
	answered
turn around	

3 Choose and write.

1 live / lived — Dinosaurs lived ________ millions of years ago.

2 notice / noticed — Tara ________ a big dinosaur.

3 shout / shouted — Todd ________ to Tara.

4 pressed / press — Todd ________ the button on the watch.

5 answer / answered — Can you ________ this question?

6 jumped / jumping — Stig ________ into Tara's arms.

1 Look and complete using the past tense.

1 He bought (buy) a ticket.

2 She ______ (be) scared.

3 He ______ (throw) the ball.

4 They ______ (leave) the house.

5 They ______ (drink) lemonade.

6 She ______ (eat) some crisps.

2 Write the sentences using the past tense.

1 I open the door. I opened the door.

2 We go to the cinema. ______

3 He drinks a cola. ______

4 She buys some popcorn. ______

5 They see a scary dinosaur. ______

1 **Think of animals in each group. Then draw them or cut pictures from magazines or use stickers.**

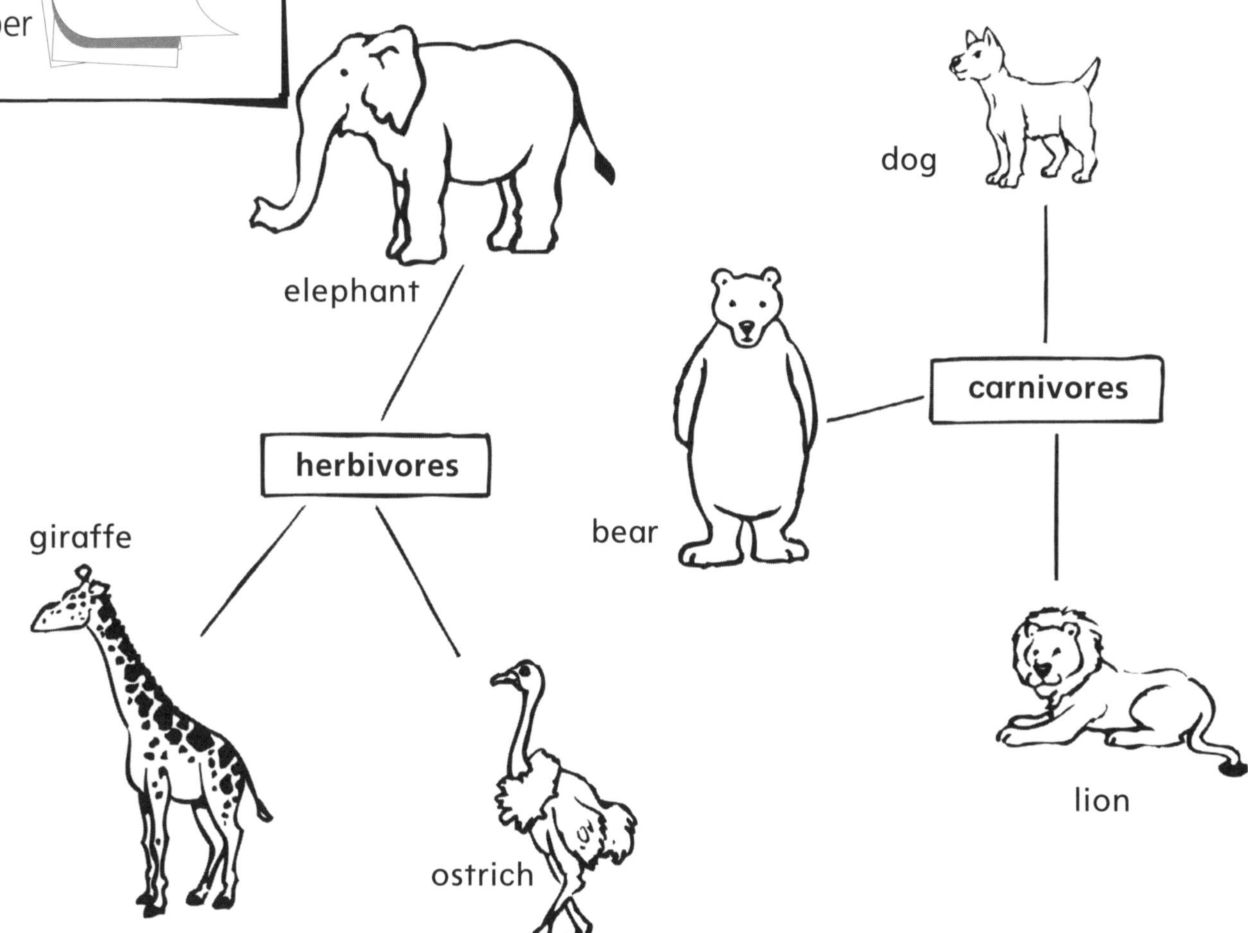

2 **Look at your poster. Can you find three animals ...**

	Animal 1	Animal 2	Animal 3
... with sharp teeth?			
... that eat plants?			
... that live in big groups?			

1 Write. Then tick (✓).

bought ate played collected went ~~drank~~

1 he drank

- a cola ✓
- some milk ☐
- some orange juice ☐

2 ____________

- an apple ☐
- an ice cream ☐
- a pizza ☐

3 ____________

- to the beach ☐
- to the river ☐
- to the museum ☐

4 ____________

- football ☐
- volleyball ☐
- tennis ☐

5 ____________

- plants ☐
- shells ☐
- fossils ☐

6 ____________

- a hat ☐
- a T-shirt ☐
- some sunglasses ☐

2 Answer the questions.

1. Did Joe drink a cola? Yes, he did.
2. Did Cleo eat an apple? ____________
3. Did Ken go to the beach? ____________
4. Did Sophie play football? ____________
5. Did Joe collect shells? ____________
6. Did Sophie buy a hat? ____________

1 Tick (✓) *true* or *false*. Then find the secret word.

		true		false	
1	Mary Anning lived in England.	☐	f	☐	m
2	Her family didn't live by the sea.	☐	u	☐	o
3	Her family was rich.	☐	t	☐	s
4	She found an enormous fossil.	☐	s	☐	a
5	She didn't become famous.	☐	b	☐	i
6	The ichthyosaurus was her first important discovery.	☐	l	☐	f
7	She was 22 when she found a plesiosaurus.	☐	s	☐	t

2 Imagine you are Mary Anning and answer the questions.

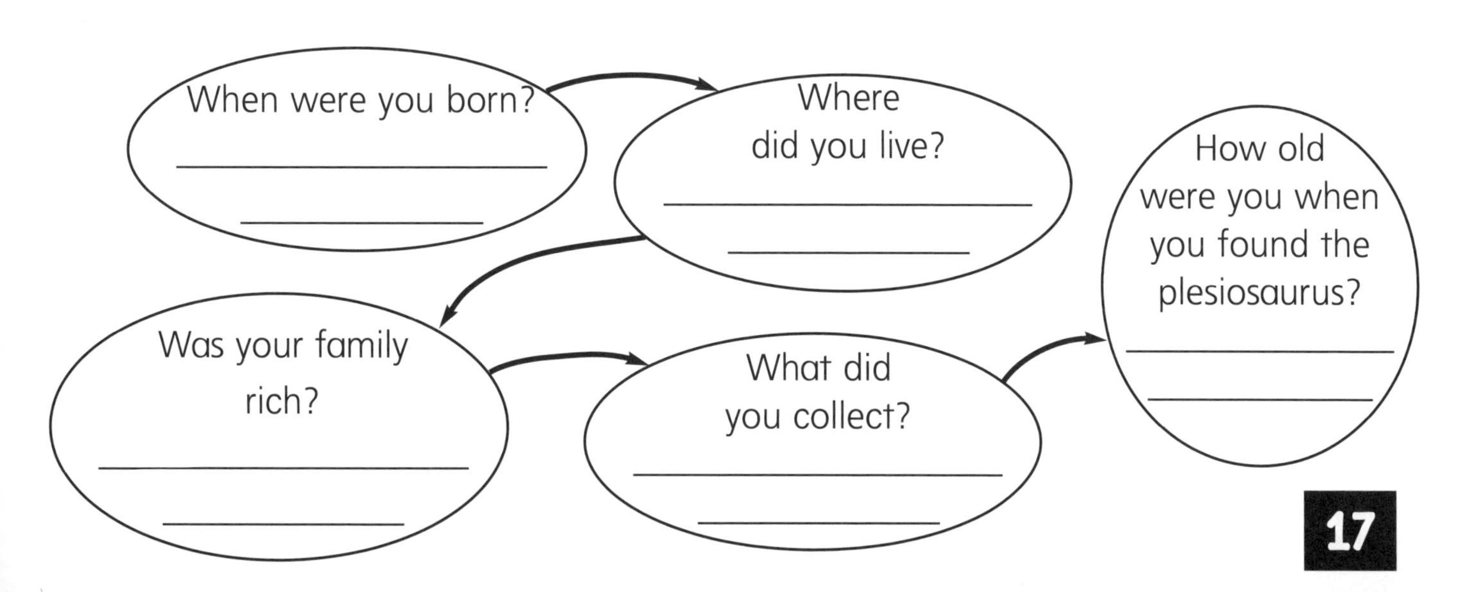

Phonics

1 Read.

Jim and Katy had two **bl**ankets.

They wanted to **pl**ay.

2 Write *bl* or *pl* to match the words in the story.

1 __ __ ue **3** __ __ ants **5** __ __ anket

2 __ __ anet **4** __ __ ack **6** __ __ ease

3 Look at the story and number the sentences.

1 I'm a blue plesiosaurus. [3]

2 Don't play on my plants, please. [ ]

3 Let's play. [ ]

4 I have a black blanket. [ ]

Try It!

LESSON 8
UNIT 2

1 Answer the questions.

1 Did some dinosaurs have wings? Yes, they did.

2 Do Tara and Todd have horns? ______________________

3 Do Tara and Todd like Stig the dinosaur? ______________________

4 Did Mary Anning live in the USA? ______________________

5 Did she collect fossils? ______________________

6 Does Todd have a magic watch? ______________________

7 Does Tara have scales? ______________________

2 Complete the sentences with the past tense of the verbs.

1 Some dinosaurs were herbivores. They ate plants. (eat)

4 Mary Anning ____________ a brother called Joseph. (have)

2 Todd ____________ the ball and Tara caught it. (throw)

5 The cat was scared. It ____________ into the tree. (jump)

3 Dinosaurs ____________ millions of years ago. (live)

6 I ____________ awake and watched a film on TV. (stay)

The Challenge

1 Look and match.

1 Fish have scales.

a 

2 Lions are carnivores. They have sharp teeth.

b 

3 The triceratops was a dinosaur with horns.

c 

4 Eagles have wings and sharp beaks.

d 

5 The stegosaurus was a dinosaur with spikes.

e 

6 Elephants are herbivores.

f 

2 Write.

1 The names of two dinosaurs: ____________________ ____________________

2 The names of two carnivores: ____________________ ____________________

3 The names of two herbivores: ____________________ ____________________

4 Four regular past tense verbs *-ed*: __________ __________ __________ __________

5 Four irregular past tense verbs: __________ __________ __________ __________

3 Find the answers and complete Tara's message.

1	What did Mary Anning collect?	butterflies	☐	Where
		fossils	☐	My
2	What do herbivores eat?	plants	☐	superhero
		meat	☐	do
3	Which animal has sharp teeth?	an eagle	☐	you
		a lion	☐	is
4	A lion is bigger than	a mouse.	☐	Spider-Man.
		a hippo.	☐	live?

Collect the correct words.

_______ _______ _______ _______

What about you?

4 Find the odd one out. Then write sentences.

1	did	had	do	was
2	went	ate	played	visit
3	watch	eat	bought	collect
4	answer	asked	shouted	jumped
5	thought	lived	walked	go

1 What / you / last weekend? What did you do last weekend?

2 Who / he / yesterday? ____________________

3 I / a dog / at the shop. ____________________

4 Did / she / the question? ____________________

5 Where / you / yesterday? ____________________

LESSON 1 UNIT

3 The Feast

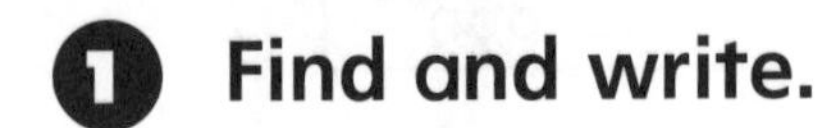

1 Find and write.

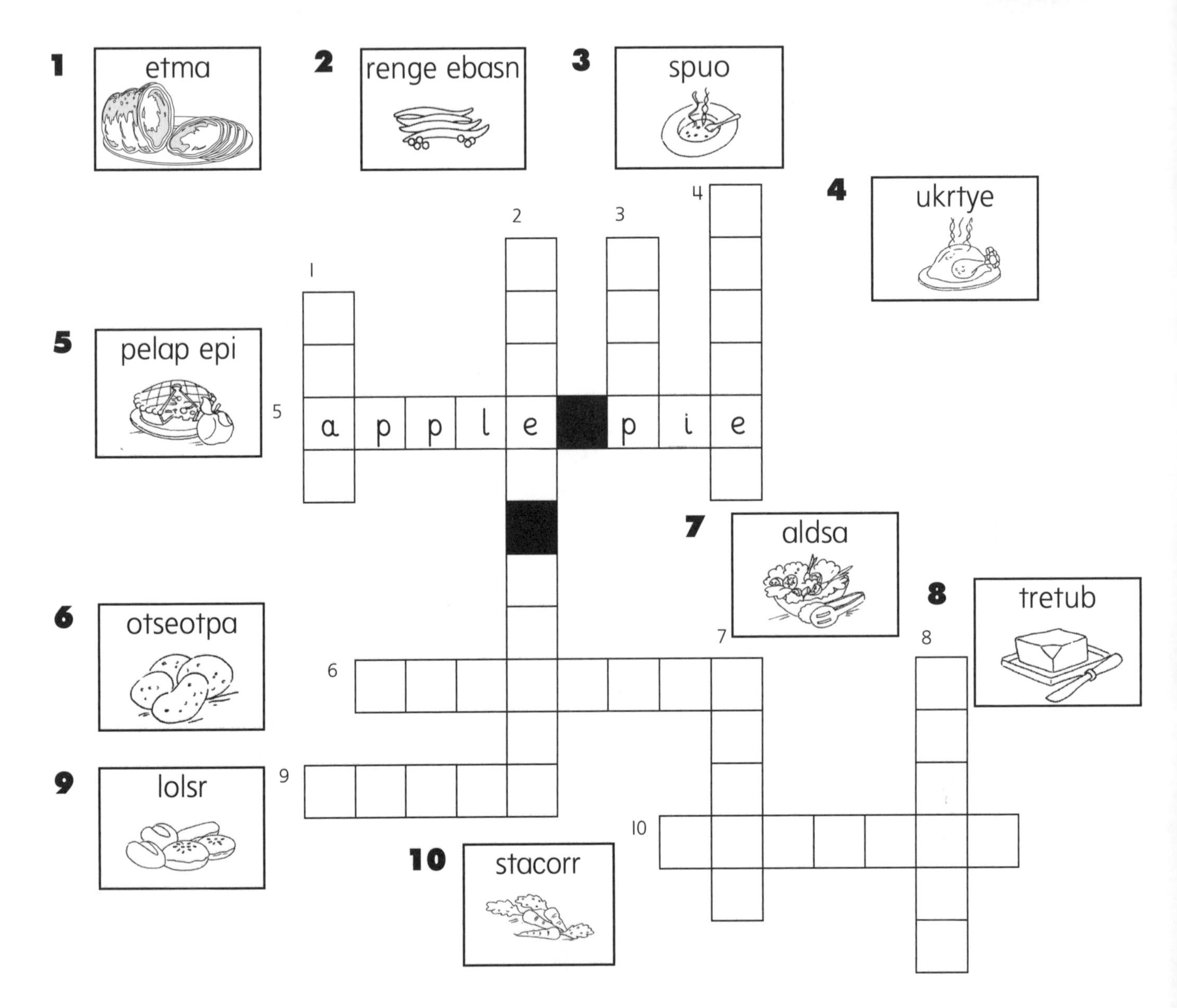

2 Write your three favourite foods from Activity I.

What about you?

1 ______________ 2 ______________ 3 ______________

1 Look and write.

+ = could − = couldn't

play football

1 Ken and Cleo were sad because ...
(−) they couldn't play football.

see a hot air balloon

2 Sophie was excited because ...
(+) ______________________

smell the turkey

3 Joe was hungry because ...
(+) ______________________

write e-mails

4 Joe and Sophie were sad because ...
(−) ______________________

run

5 Ken was bored because ...
(−) ______________________

climb the tree

6 Cleo was happy because ...
(+) ______________________

2 Look and complete using *could* or *couldn't*.

1 She ______________ swim.
2 She ______________ run.
3 She ______________ read.
4 She ______________ climb trees.

LESSON 3 UNIT 3

1 Write the opposites.

1 I couldn't climb a tree. I could climb a tree.
2 I could swim. ______
3 I could walk. ______
4 I couldn't talk. ______
5 I couldn't run. ______
6 I could tie my shoe. ______

What about you? 2 Write using *I could* or *I couldn't*.

What could you do when you were five?

1 ______ swim.
2 ______ speak English.
3 ______ ride a bike.
4 ______ use a computer.
5 ______ count to 10.
6 ______ make my bed.
7 ______ wash my hair.
8 ______ help my mum and dad.
9 ______ run.
10 ______ stand on one leg.

How many things could you do? ☐

How many things couldn't you do? ☐

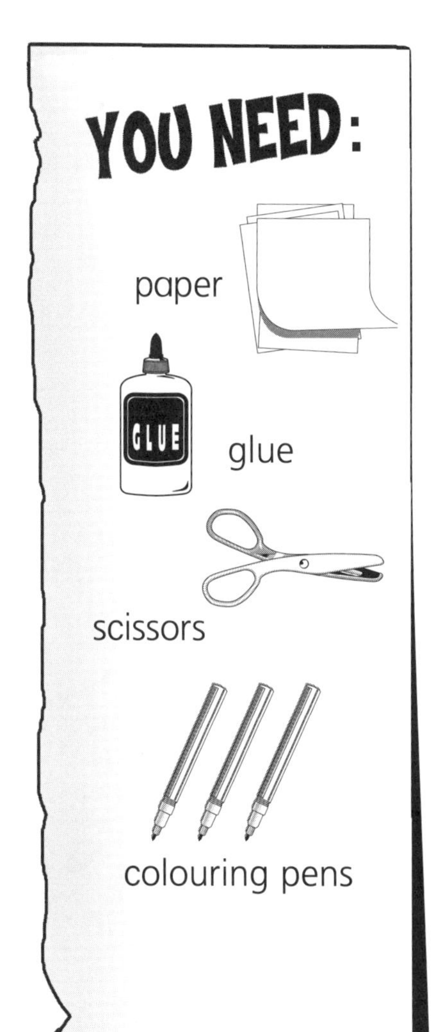

1 Decorate a piece of paper with colours, glitter, stickers, etc.

2 Fold the piece of paper in half.

3 Cut lines along the fold.

4 Open up the paper and stick the ends together.

5 Cut another thin strip of paper for the handle. Glue it on to the lantern.

LESSON 5 UNIT 3

1 Write the questions. Then look and match.

1 some	8 cake	15 window
2 open	9 have	16 you
3 wash	10 your	17 the
4 I	11 more	18 on
5 take	12 play	19 computer
6 could	13 hands	20 please
7 with	14 my	21 picture

1 6 4 12 7 16 20?
Could I play with you, please? f

2 6 4 5 10 21 20?
_______________ ☐

3 6 4 3 14 13 20?
_______________ ☐

4 6 16 2 17 15 20?
_______________ ☐

5 6 4 12 18 10 19 20?
_______________ ☐

6 6 4 9 1 11 8 20?
_______________ ☐

2 Choose and write.

Where would you hear these questions?

in the park at school at home

1 Could you clean your room, please? _______________

2 Could you look at question 1, please? _______________

3 Could you throw the ball, please? _______________

1 Complete the chart.

What could people do in 1880? What couldn't they do?

fly in planes play football send e-mails read newspapers
go on holiday watch TV go on a picnic drive a car use a laptop
go to the theatre swim in the sea play computer games

People could ...	People couldn't ...
______________	______________
______________	______________
______________	______________
______________	______________
______________	______________
______________	______________

2 Now write five things about your parents.

What could they do when they were young? What couldn't they do?

1 ______________________________

2 ______________________________

3 ______________________________

4 ______________________________

5 ______________________________

Phonics

1 Read.

Sometimes Uncle Mac is **sl**y!

2 Write *fl* or *sl* to match the words in the story.

1 __ __ oat 3 __ __ ip 5 __ __ ippers

2 __ __ eep 4 __ __ ute 6 __ __ oor

3 Look at the story and complete the sentences.

1 I can make a flute float .

2 And you can ______ .

3 She's going ______ !

4 Could you ______ ?

Try It!

LESSON 8 UNIT 3

1 Look and write. What could / couldn't they do two years ago?

write speak English read ride a bike run ~~swim~~

1 She could swim.

2 __________

3 __________

4 __________

5 __________

6 __________

2 Look and write.

When I was five ...	yes	no
I could read.	✓	
I could ride a horse.		✓
I could swim.		✓
I could speak English.	✓	

1 Could he read? __________

2 __________ ride a horse? __________

3 __________ swim? __________

4 __________ speak English? __________

The Challenge

1 Solve the puzzle. Then look and match.

1 [e] meat meat	2 [ ] ____ rolls	3 [ ] ____ soup	4 [ ] ____ salad
5 [ ] ____ butter	6 [ ] ____ potatoes	7 [ ] ____ turkey	8 [ ] ____ carrots

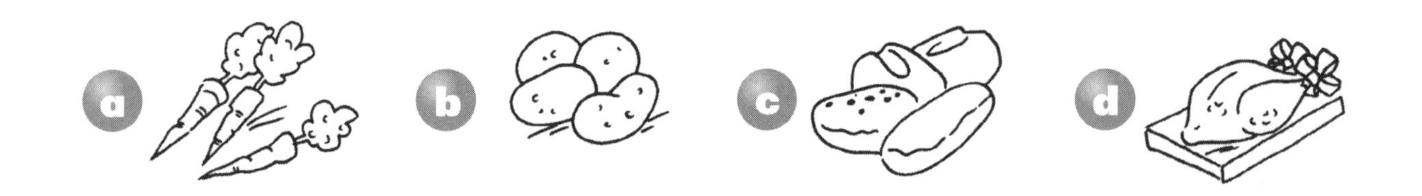

2 Put the questions in order.

1 door / you / open / Could / the Could you open the door, please?

2 you / me / help / Could ______________________, please?

3 laptop / I / use / Could / your ______________________, please?

4 I / Could / more / some / have / cake ______________________, please?

5 hands / wash / I / Could / my ______________________, please?

6 tonight / you / me / Could / call ______________________, please?

3 Tick (✓) the words to complete Tara's message.

1	Which month is Ramadan?	ninth	☐	My
		third	☐	I
2	People eat sohour before	sunset.	☐	couldn't
		sunrise.	☐	favourite
3	They eat iftar after	sunrise.	☐	swim
		sunset.	☐	festival
4	They break the fast with	cakes.	☐	very
		dates.	☐	is
5	A fanous is a special	lantern.	☐	Halloween.
		soup.	☐	well.

Collect the correct words.

_______ _______ _______ _______ _______

What about you?

4 Make word crosses.

1

c
o p e n
u
l
d o o r

2

f
a
r s
c o _ l d n' _
n

3

f
i
_ o u p
h

Now write sentences using each word cross.

1 Could you open the door, please?

2 ____________________

3 ____________________

At the Party

1 Find, complete and draw.

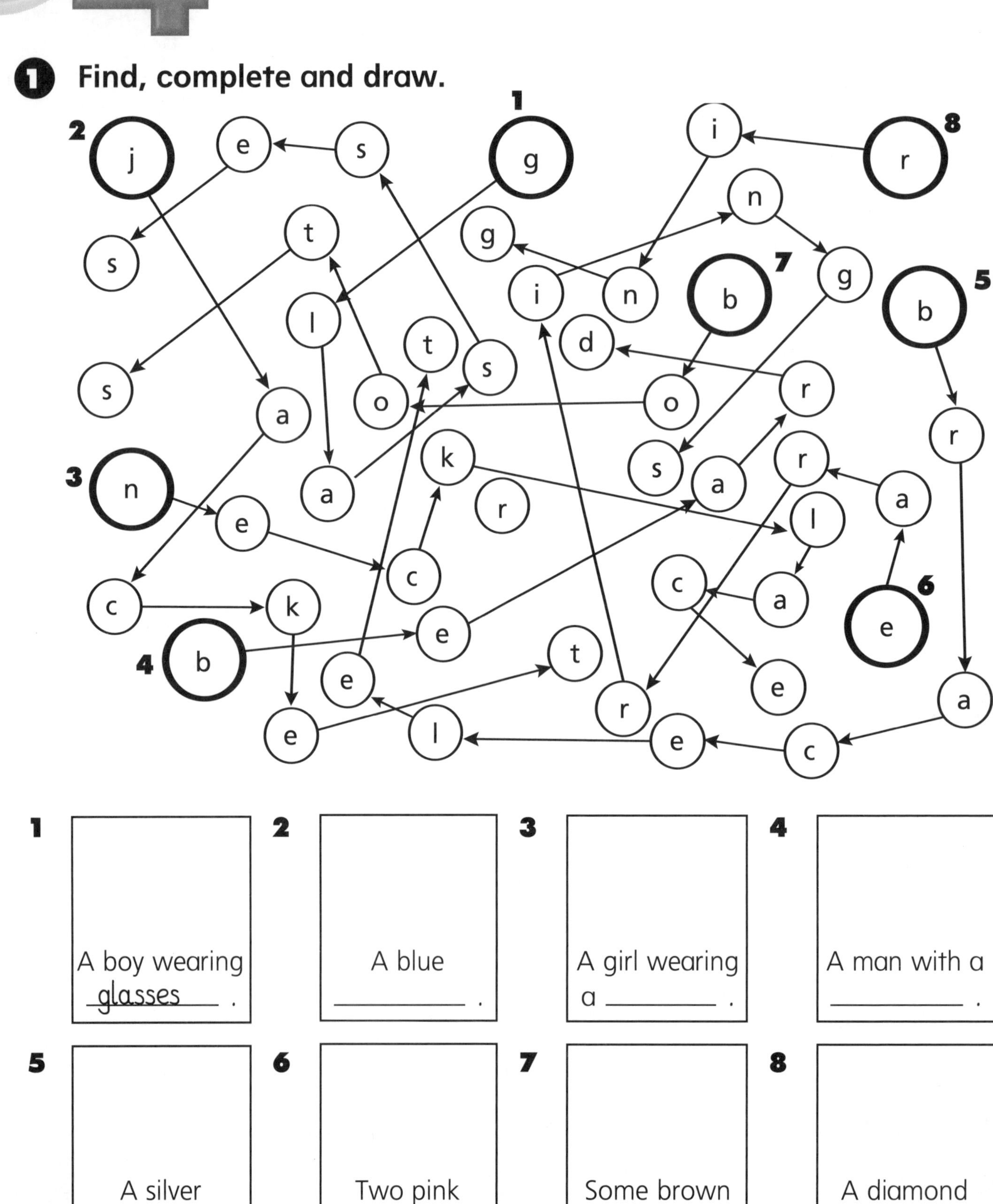

1 Write.

1 She used to be rich.
She's poor now.

2 He __________ have a beard.
He doesn't have __________ now.

3 She __________ live in the city.
She lives in the __________ now.

4 He __________ be sad.
He's __________ now.

2 What about you? Write sentences about yourself using *used to*.

1 I used to have __________, but I don't have one now.

2 I used to eat __________, but I don't __________ now.

3 I used to watch __________ on TV, but I don't __________ now.

4 I used to play __________, but I don't __________ now.

5 I used to like __________, but I don't __________ now.

1 Match.

1 They used to grow their vegetables. ☐

2 They used to build their homes. ☐

3 They used to light fires. ☐

4 They used to wear boots. ☐

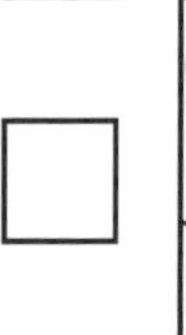

2 Look and write what they used to do.

skip

jump

1 She used to skip.

2 ______________________

3 ______________________

4 ______________________

Project

Make a CD Holder

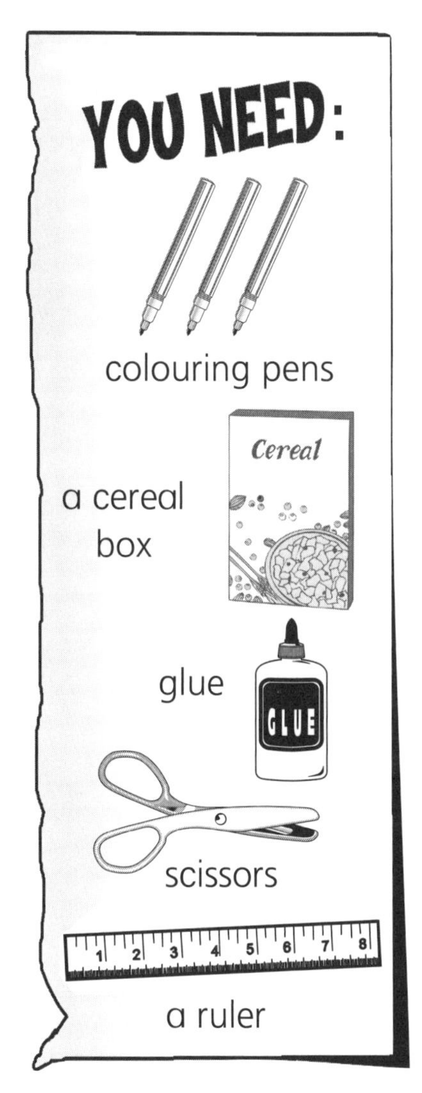

Make a CD holder and keep all your favourite music in it!

1 Cut a rectangle from the cereal box.

2 Fold the two sides into the middle and glue the ends together.

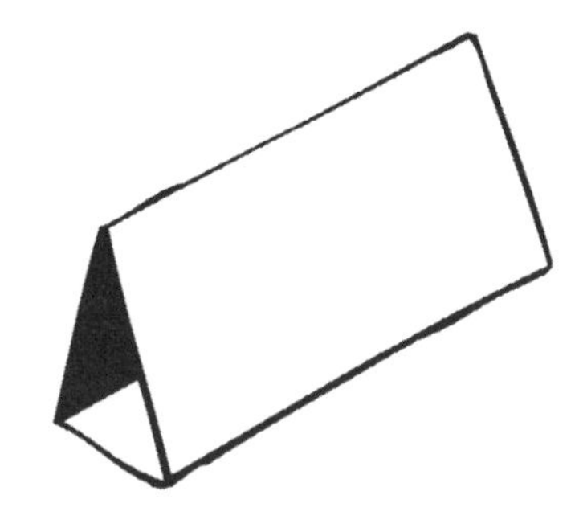

3 Draw lines 3 cm. apart and 4 cm. from the edge.

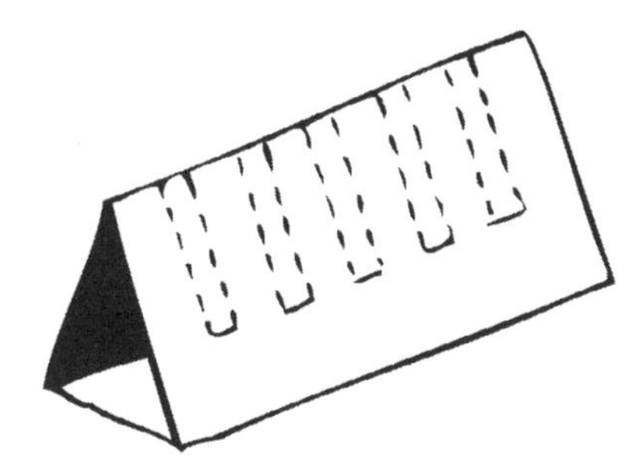

4 Cut along the lines.

5 Decorate your CD holder.

6 Keep your CDs safe.

LESSON 5 UNIT 4

1 Look and write.

2 Complete the chart.

My Class			
have a bike now		used to have a bike	
play with dolls now		used to play with dolls	
drink milk now		used to drink milk	
like sweets now		used to like sweets	
wear nappies now		used to wear nappies	

How many people used to have a bike but now don't have one?

Ken

1 Read and write.

150 years ago ...

People didn't use to have **1** cars, they used to **2** __________. They didn't have **3** __________, they used to read **4** __________.

They didn't use to buy **5** __________, they used to make it.

People didn't use to have **6** __________, they used to write with a **7** __________.

2 Look at Activity 1. Write using *used to* (✓) or *didn't use to* (✗).

1. ✓ make / butter They used to make butter.
2. ✗ have / cars __________
3. ✓ write / pen __________
4. ✗ have / TVs __________
5. ✓ walk __________
6. ✗ buy / butter __________
7. ✗ have / laptops __________

LESSON 7 UNIT 4

Phonics

1 Read.

'I want **br**ead for **br**eakfast,' said the **pr**incess from **Br**azil. Her big **br**other gave her some **br**ead.

'I want the first **pr**ize,' said the **pr**incess from **Br**azil. Her big **br**other gave her the **pr**ize.

'I want the **br**own **pr**esent,' said the **pr**incess from **Br**azil. Her big **br**other gave her the **br**own **pr**esent.

The **pr**incess from **Br**azil opened the **br**own **pr**esent. It was a box of **br**icks!

2 Write *pr* or *br* to match the words in the story.

1 __ __ eakfast
2 __ __ ead
3 __ __ ize
4 __ __ azil
5 __ __ other
6 __ __ own
7 __ __ esent
8 __ __ incess

3 Write *true* or *false*.

1 The princess wanted bread for dinner. ____________

2 Her brother didn't give her the prize. ____________

3 The princess wanted the brown present. ____________

4 There were bricks in the box. ____________

Try It!

LESSON 8
UNIT 4

1 **Tick (✓) the true sentences.**

1 She didn't use to have a cat. ☐
She used to have a cat. ☐

2 He used to play volleyball. ☐
He used to play basketball. ☐

3 They used to play with dolls. ☐
They used to play with cars. ☐

4 He used to ride a tiger. ☐
He used to ride an elephant. ☐

2 **Write about the princess.**

She used to be rich .

She used to wear ______________________

______________________ .

She didn't use to wear ______________________

______________________ .

The Challenge

1 Find the odd one out. Then write sentences.

1	jacket	boots	skirt	swim
2	fanous	laptops	sohour	Ramadan
3	breakfast	Brazil	present	brown
4	ate	buy	ran	lived
5	swimming	playing football	running	read
6	have	liked	saw	bought

1 He / used to / sea ______________________

2 People / didn't use to / have ______________________

3 Tom / wanted / birthday ______________________

4 I / used to / sweets ______________________

5 They / used to / history books ______________________

6 She / used to / a pet rabbit ______________________

2 Find the question. Then write your answer.

= to = you = play = Are = wearing

= swim = used = glasses?

ring necklace earrings hat

Question: ____________ ____________ ____________ ____________ ?

Your answer: ______________________________

3 Tick (✓) the words to complete Tara's message.

1	People didn't use to have	beards.	☐	Ronaldo
		laptops.	☐	I
2	Where do you wear a bracelet?	On your arm.	☐	was
		On your head.	☐	is
3	People used to	drive cars.	☐	a
		ride horses.	☐	born
4	People didn't use to have	trucks.	☐	in
		beds.	☐	famous
5	Where do you wear boots?	Around your neck.	☐	footballer.
		On your feet.	☐	Brazil.

Collect the correct words.

_______ _______ _______ _______ _______

What about you?

4 What comes next?

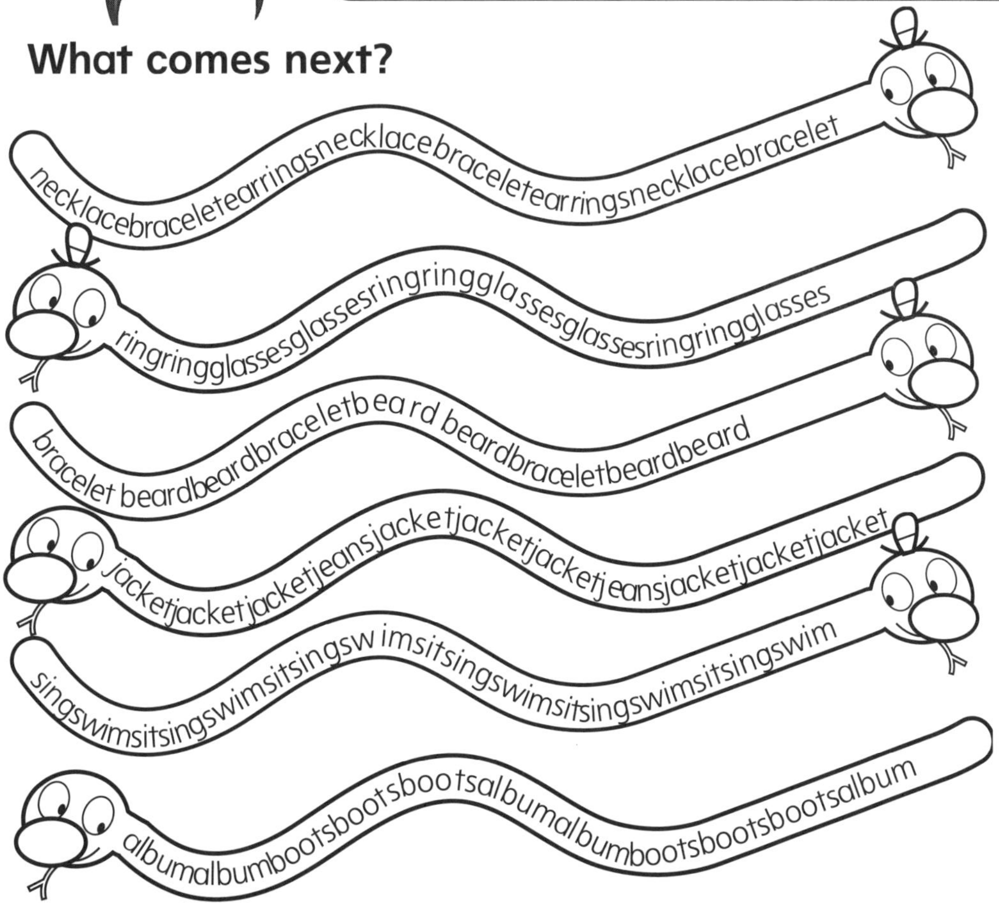

1 necklacebraceletearringsnecklacebraceletearringsnecklacebracelet earrings

2 ringringglassesglassesringringglassesglassesringringglasses ________

3 bracelet beardbeardbraceletbeard beardbraceletbeardbeard ________

4 jacketjacketjacketjeansjacketjacketjacketjeansjacketjacketjacket ________

5 singswimsitsingswimsitsingswimsitsingswimsitsingswim ________

6 albumalbumbootsbootsalbumalbumbootsbootsalbum ________

5 At the Farm

1 Find and write the labels.

hedge	goat	horse	sheep	cock	barn	cow	hay	gate

2 Read and colour the picture.

The goat is brown. The cock is black and red. The horse is grey. The cow is black and white. The sheep is white. The barn is red and brown. The hay is yellow and the hedge is green.

1 Look and tick (✓). Then write.

1 cocks		2 sheep		3 goats		4 cows	
flying	☐	sleeping	☐	eating	☐	running	☐
singing	☐	hiding	☐	jumping	☐	drinking	☐
sleeping	☐	playing	☐	sitting down	☐	playing	☐

1 The cocks were ______________________

2 ______________________

3 ______________________

4 ______________________

2 Look and write. Then draw.

The 1 ________ ________ chasing the 2 ________. The 3 ________ ________ sleeping next to the 4 ________.

The 5 ________ ________ eating 6 ________.

1 Write the opposites.

was → wasn't were → weren't

1 He was eating some bread. ____________________

2 It was strange. ____________________

3 We weren't drinking lemonade. ____________________

4 They were playing chess. ____________________

5 We were doing karate. ____________________

6 The cows were eating hay. ____________________

7 She wasn't wearing a dress. ____________________

8 He wasn't listening to music. ____________________

2 Write *was* or *were*.

1 The cows ____________ sleeping.

2 The horse ____________ eating.

3 The farmer ____________ running.

4 Two horses ____________ chasing a dog.

3 Find and write. Then tick (✓) the correct picture.

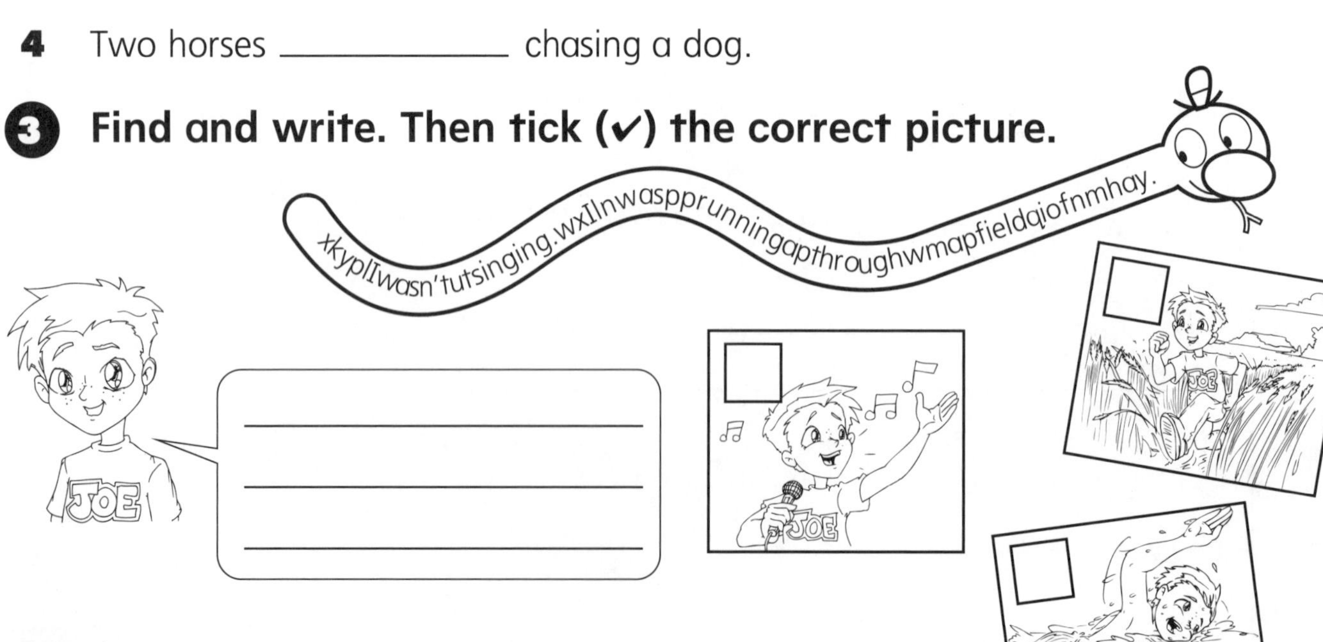

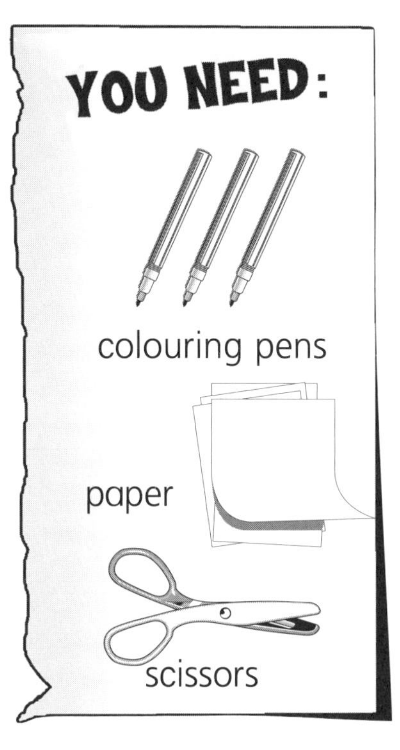

1 **Write about a favourite story.**

____

____

____

____

____

2 **Make a class display.**

1 Take a sheet of paper and trace this picture twice.

2 Choose two characters from your favourite story. Then draw them on your pictures.

3 Cut out your pictures.

4 Stick your characters on the wall.

LESSON 5 UNIT 5

1 Read and answer. (What about you?)

1 What were you doing at 6 o'clock last night?

____

2 What was your friend doing last Saturday?

____

3 What were you doing ten minutes ago?

____

4 Was your teacher reading at seven o'clock last night?

____

5 Were you studying English an hour ago?

____

2 Find the verbs. Then complete the questions using *was* and *were*.

a	e	a	t	i	n	g	i	g
p	l	a	y	i	n	g	l	p
d	i	r	i	d	i	n	g	n
l	p	p	l	a	y	i	n	g
w	r	i	t	i	n	g	w	r
k	t	a	k	i	n	g	t	n
g	a	g	g	o	i	n	g	n
w	a	t	c	h	i	n	g	w
a	p	a	i	n	t	i	n	g
t	a	l	k	i	n	g	l	k

1 ______ the cow ______ hay?
2 ______ you ______ the recorder?
3 ______ they ______ white horses?
4 ______ she ______ chess?
5 ______ he ______ an e-mail?
6 ______ they ______ the bus?
7 ______ you ______ to the shop?
8 ______ the dog ______ the sheep?
9 ______ the farmer ______ the barn?
10 ______ they ______ on the phone?

1 Write your own story. Draw a picture.

At ____________ o'clock yesterday, I was walking in the ____________. I was thinking about ____________. I was eating ____________ and I was drinking ____________. Suddenly, I saw a ____________. I was really scared, so I ____________ home!

What about you? 2 Write another story.

Phonics

1 Read.

One day **Tr**udi **dr**essed and **dr**ove to the country.

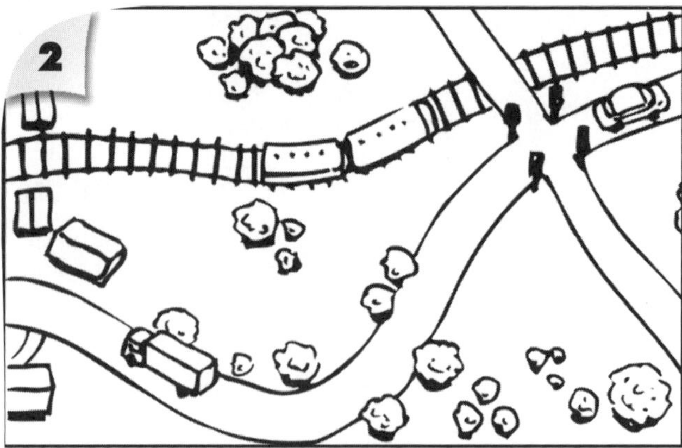

She passed **tr**ains, **tr**ees and **tr**affic lights.

She saw a farmer **dr**iving a **tr**actor. She saw a sheep sleeping under a **tr**ee.

It was a great **tr**ip.

2 Write *dr* or *tr* to match the words in the story.

1 __ __ essed
2 __ __ ees
3 __ __ iving
4 __ __ ains
5 __ __ affic lights
6 __ __ actor
7 __ __ ove
8 __ __ ip

3 Look at the story and number the sentences.

1 She saw a farmer driving a tractor. ☐
2 Trudi drove to the country. ☐
3 She passed trains and trees. ☐
4 It was a great trip. ☐

Try It!

LESSON 8
UNIT 5

1 Find and write. What were they doing last night?

1. ______________________
2. ______________________
3. ______________________
4. ______________________
5. She was riding a horse.
6. ______________________

2 Write.

LOOK at your wordlist

1.  The horse was jumping the __________ .
2.  The __________ was eating an __________ .
3.  The __________ was chasing the __________ .
4.  The __________ were eating the __________ .
5.  The __________ were asleep in the __________ .
6.  The __________ was behind the __________ .

The Challenge

1 Find the words and match.

1 etga ____________ [f]

2 rbna ____________ [ ]

3 tago ____________ [ ]

4 eghed ____________ [ ]

5 woc ____________ [ ]

6 epehs ____________ [ ]

7 serho ____________ [ ]

c

a 

b 

d 

e 

f 

g 

2 Find the differences and write.

picture A

picture B

In picture A, a sheep is hiding behind the hedge.

____.

In picture B, ____

____.

3 Tick (✓) the words to complete Tara's message.

1	Horses and sheep are	carnivores.	☐	He
		herbivores.	☐	Last
2	It's good to lie.	true	☐	doesn't
		false	☐	night
3	Which word rhymes with 'drive'?	life	☐	like
		dive	☐	I
4	Sheep usually live in	a field.	☐	was
		a house.	☐	the
5	A lion has sharp	teeth.	☐	reading.
		spikes.	☐	rain.

Collect the correct words.

______ ______ ___ ______ ______

What were you doing?

What about you? 4 Complete the chart. Which animals do you like?

cats birds crocodiles cheetahs goats horses dogs sheep monkeys jellyfish

I love ... | I like ... | I don't like ...

wolves hippos snakes bears starfish lions giraffes cocks dolphins cows

LESSON 1

UNIT 6

In the Shop

1 Tick (✓) the correct words.

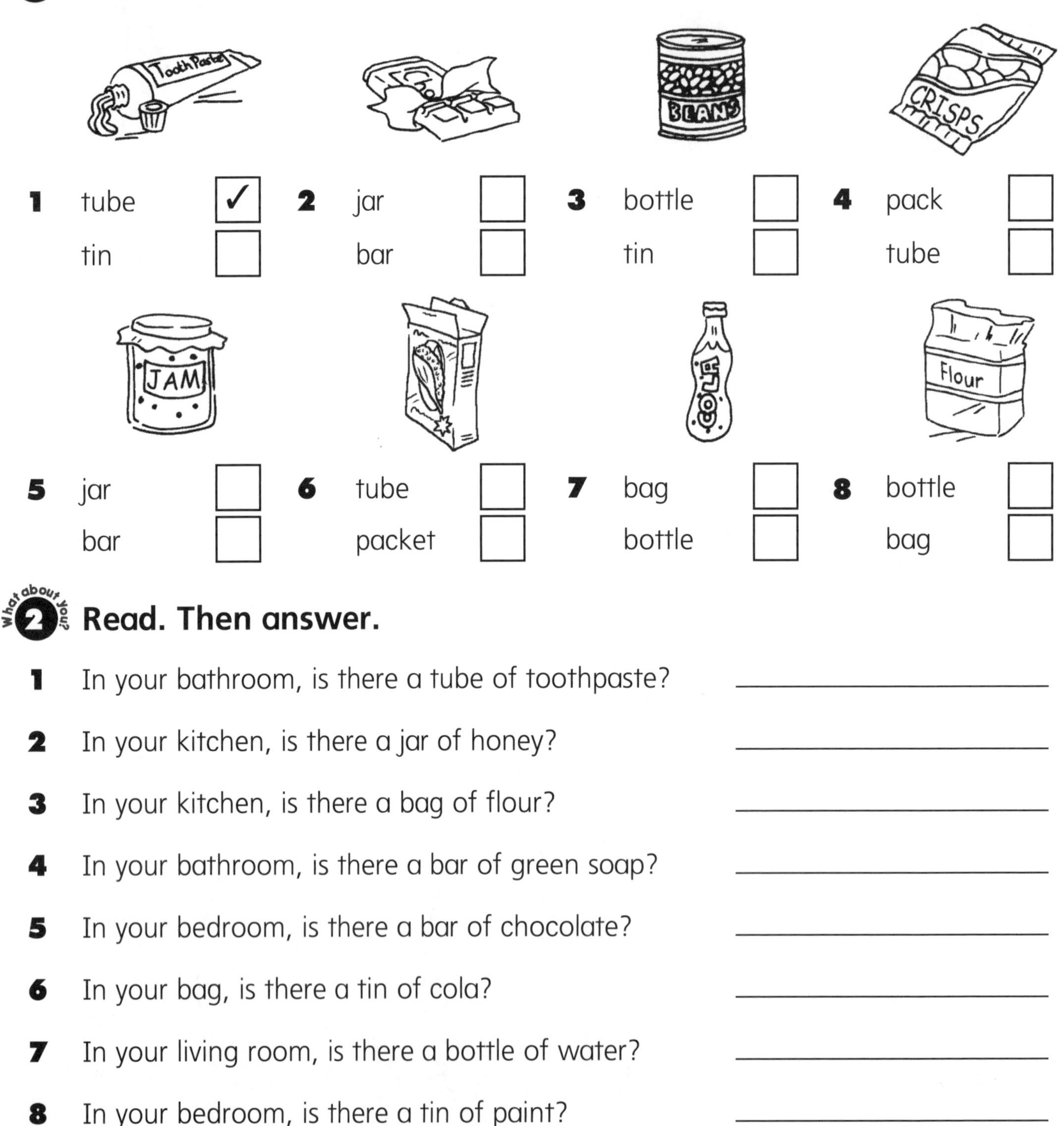

1 tube ✓
tin

2 jar
bar

3 bottle
tin

4 pack
tube

5 jar
bar

6 tube
packet

7 bag
bottle

8 bottle
bag

What about you? 2 Read. Then answer.

1 In your bathroom, is there a tube of toothpaste? ______________

2 In your kitchen, is there a jar of honey? ______________

3 In your kitchen, is there a bag of flour? ______________

4 In your bathroom, is there a bar of green soap? ______________

5 In your bedroom, is there a bar of chocolate? ______________

6 In your bag, is there a tin of cola? ______________

7 In your living room, is there a bottle of water? ______________

8 In your bedroom, is there a tin of paint? ______________

What about you? 1 Write.

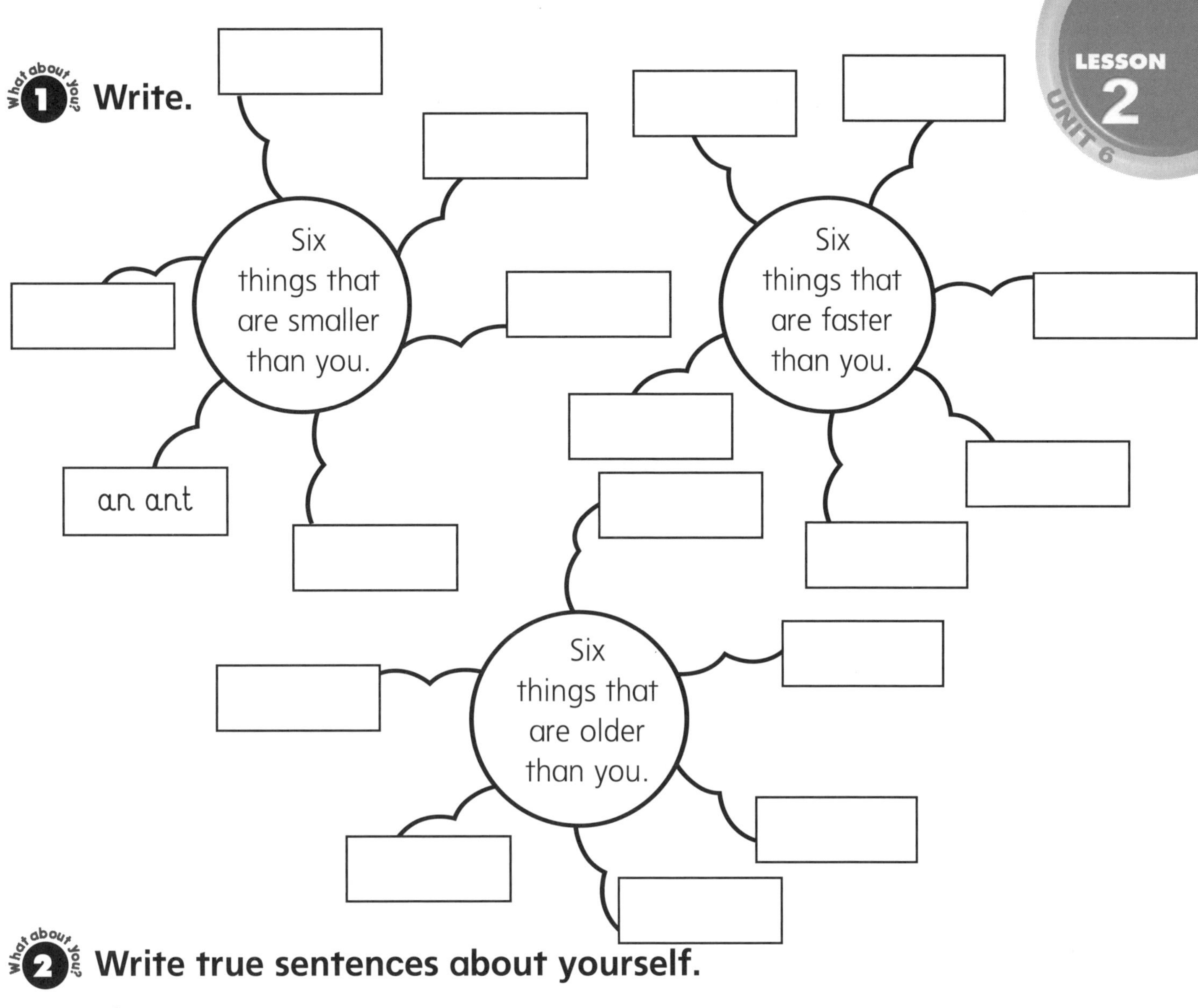

What about you? 2 Write true sentences about yourself.

1 I'm smaller than ______________ .
2 ______ faster than ______________ .
3 ______ older than ______________ .
4 ______ larger than ______________ .
5 ______ fatter than ______________ .
6 ______ thinner than ______________ .
7 ______ taller than ______________ .
8 ______ younger than ______________ .

1 Write about your superhero. Then draw.

What about you?

Who is your superhero?

____

braver	faster	bigger
smaller	smarter	

____

____

____

____

____

2 Look and write.

b

c

d

1 **a** is bigger (big) and stronger (strong) than **b**.

2 **b** is __________ (small) and __________ (fast) than **a**.

3 **c** is __________ (tall) than **b** and __________ (thin) than **d**.

4 **d** is __________ (fat) and __________ (short) than **c**.

5 **d** is __________ (fat) than **b** and __________ (short) than **a**.

6 **a** is __________ (big) than **c** and __________ (tall) than **d**.

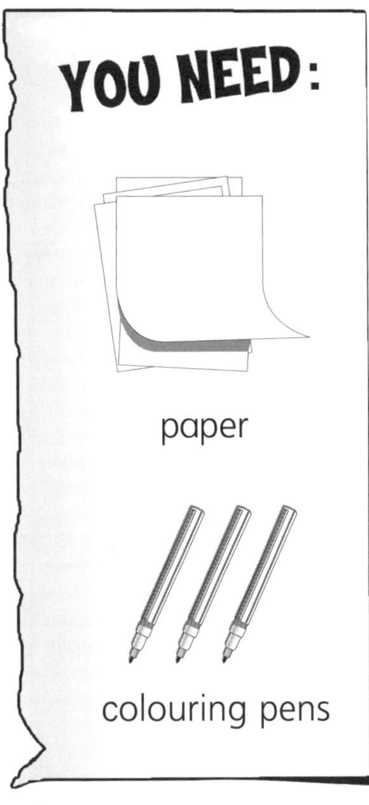

1 Look and match.

1 a dirty T-shirt
2 a short line
3 a small circle
4 a big square
5 a thin mouse
6 a long flower

2 Fold two pieces of paper in half.

3 Copy the pictures onto the paper. Label the pictures A. Leave a space under each picture.

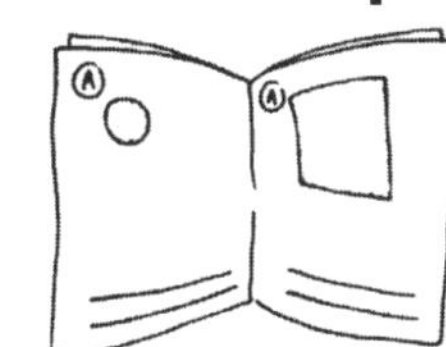

4 Draw another picture on each page. Colour then label the pictures B.

1 Draw a cleaner T-shirt.
2 Draw a longer line.
3 Draw a bigger circle.
4 Draw a smaller square.
5 Draw a fatter mouse.
6 Draw a shorter flower.

My Revision Booklet

5 Write.

smaller shorter bigger taller cleaner dirtier longer thinner fatter

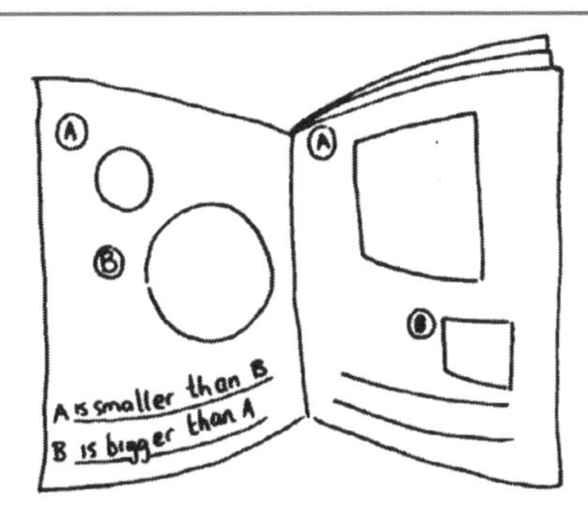

LESSON 5 UNIT 6

1 Choose and tick (✓). Then write.

What are you going to buy?

1

a jar of ...	
jam	☐
peanuts	☐
chillies	☐
olives	✓

2

a bar of ...	
soap	☐
chocolate	☐

3

a tin of ...	
beans	☐
tomatoes	☐
carrots	☐

4

a pack of ...	
crisps	☐
biscuits	☐
butter	☐
cereal	☐

5

a bag of ...	
flour	☐
sugar	☐
rice	☐

6

a bottle of ...	
cola	☐
orange juice	☐
lemonade	☐
water	☐

1 I'd like a jar of olives, please.

2 ______

3 ______

4 ______

5 ______

6 ______

2 Number the sentences to make a dialogue. Then write.

☐ Here you are.

☐ It's fifty pence.

☐ Thank you. Goodbye.

1 Good morning. Can I help you?

☐ How much is that?

☐ Yes, I'd like a pack of crisps, please.

1 Good morning. Can I help you?

2 ______

3 ______

4 ______

5 ______

6 ______

1 Write true sentences.

What would you like?

1 newer ______________________

2 better ______________________

3 faster ______________________

4 larger ______________________

5 smaller ______________________

6 more comfortable ______________________

2 Answer.

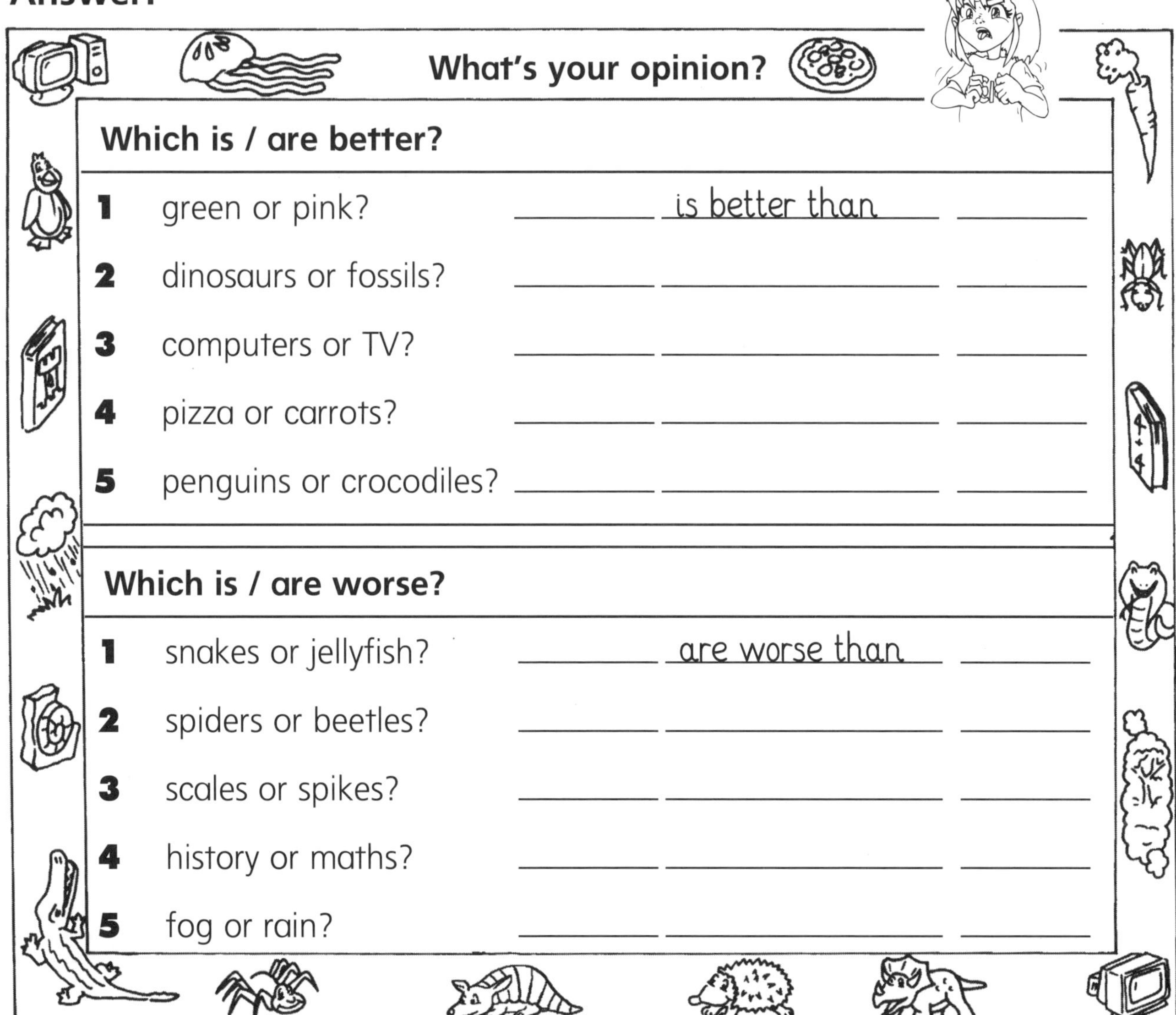

What's your opinion?

Which is / are better?

1 green or pink? ________ is better than ________

2 dinosaurs or fossils? ________ ________ ________

3 computers or TV? ________ ________ ________

4 pizza or carrots? ________ ________ ________

5 penguins or crocodiles? ________ ________ ________

Which is / are worse?

1 snakes or jellyfish? ________ are worse than ________

2 spiders or beetles? ________ ________ ________

3 scales or spikes? ________ ________ ________

4 history or maths? ________ ________ ________

5 fog or rain? ________ ________ ________

Phonics

1 Read.

1 **Gr**ippy **gr**ew **gr**een **gr**apes in the **gr**eenhouse.

2 **Gr**uppy **gr**ew **gr**een **gr**ass.

3 They ate **gr**een **gr**apes and **gr**ass with ice **cr**eam and **gr**avy!

4 The clowns are **cr**azy!

2 Write *gr* or *cr* to match the words in the story.

1	__ __ ippy	**4**	__ __ apes	**7**	__ __ eam
2	__ __ azy	**5**	__ __ ew	**8**	__ __ avy
3	__ __ eenhouse	**6**	__ __ ass	**9**	__ __ een

3 Write *true* or *false*.

1 Gruppy grew green grass. ____________

2 Grippy likes ice cream and gravy. ____________

3 Gruppy doesn't like green grapes and grass. ____________

4 The clowns are crazy! ____________

Try It!

LESSON 8
UNIT 6

1 Tick (✓) the true sentences.

1 An elephant is smaller than a penguin. ☐

2 An ant is smaller than an egg. ☐

3 A tree is taller than a bush. ☐

4 A cow is bigger than a sheep. ☐

5 Grandma is younger than my sister. ☐

6 A horse is faster than a dog. ☐

7 A cock is stronger than a goat. ☐

8 Dinosaurs are older than people. ☐

Now correct the false sentences.

1 ______________________________

2 ______________________________

3 ______________________________

2 Choose and write.

1 bag _I'd like a bag of biscuits, please._

2 bottle ______________________________

3 tin ______________________________

4 jar ______________________________

5 packet ______________________________

6 bar ______________________________

The Challenge

1 Complete the chart.

~~sweet~~s ~~bag~~ bottle cola crisps box jelly pack
tin candles rice jar green beans tube bar flour

Supermarket Items	sweets			
Containers	bag			

2 Look at the chart in Activity I. Draw and write.

1

2

3

4

3 Tick (✓) the words to complete Tara's message.

1	Are you heavier than an elephant?	yes	☐	Last
		no	☐	I'd
2	Are you shorter than a giraffe?	yes	☐	like
		no	☐	year
3	Is a horse faster than an ant?	yes	☐	a
		no	☐	we
4	Is a bed more comfortable than a bench?	yes	☐	new
		no	☐	bought
5	Is a balloon lighter than a chair?	yes	☐	computer game.
		no	☐	biscuits.

Collect the correct words.

_______ _______ ____ _______ _______

____

What would you like to buy?

4 Find the odd sound out.

1	sleep	sheep	float	keep
2	bread	head	need	bed
3	buy	my	why	use
4	ring	sing	song	king
5	chess	cheese	dress	princess
6	green	seen	grass	cream

7 In the City

LOOK at your wordlist

1 Find and write.

1	tetaarsrun	r ________	**7**	rylro	l________
2	bezar gsorcsin	z______ c______	**8**	bsu psot	b______ s______
3	usibrbh ibn	r______ b______	**9**	sbu	b________
4	malp psto	l______ p______	**10**	wnegesant	n________
5	rca	c ________	**11**	veenmpat	p________
6	otps xbo	p______ b______	**12**	ocrmtoceyl	m________

2 Look and write.

In picture A, there's a lorry, ____________________

____

____________________ .

In picture B, ____________________

____

____________________ .

1 Choose.

1	The oldest car.	☐	a b c	
2	The dirtiest T-shirt.	☐	a b c	
3	The youngest girl.	☐	a b c	
4	The fattest cat.	☐	a b c	
5	The most beautiful flower.	☐	a b c	

2 Choose the correct word.

LOOK at your wordlist

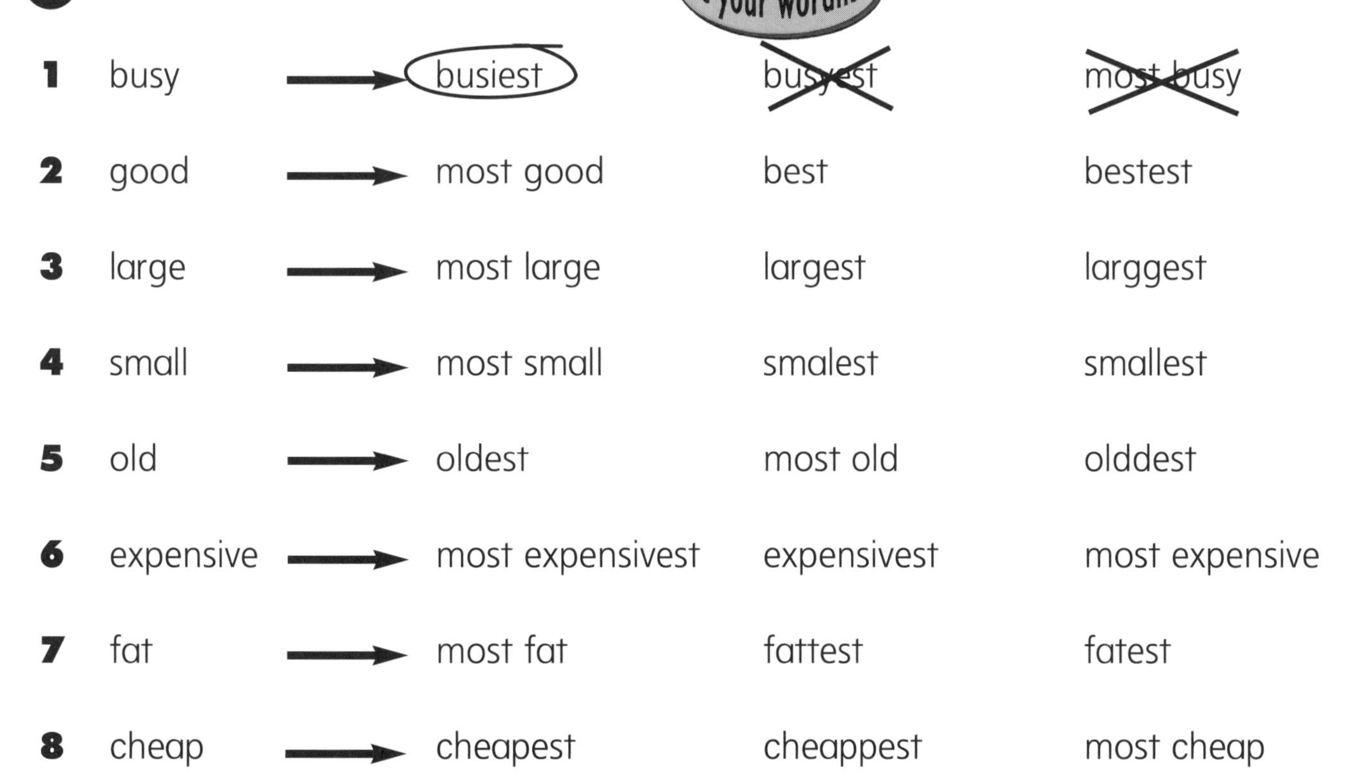

1	busy	→	busiest	~~busyest~~	~~most busy~~
2	good	→	most good	best	bestest
3	large	→	most large	largest	larggest
4	small	→	most small	smalest	smallest
5	old	→	oldest	most old	olddest
6	expensive	→	most expensivest	expensivest	most expensive
7	fat	→	most fat	fattest	fatest
8	cheap	→	cheapest	cheappest	most cheap

LESSON 3 UNIT 1

1 Match the opposites.

1	the largest	g	a	the fastest
2	the thinnest		b	the saddest
3	the slowest		c	the most boring
4	the cleanest		d	the fattest
5	the most exciting		e	the worst
6	the best		f	the noisiest
7	the happiest		g	the smallest
8	the quietest		h	the dirtiest

2 What about you? Write the answers.

1 Where is the nicest park in your town?

The nicest park in my town is ______

2 Where is the busiest street in your town?

______

3 What's the name of a shop that's open longest in your town?

______

4 Who is the friendliest person in your family?

______

5 Who is the oldest person in your family?

______

6 Who is the youngest person in your family?

______

7 Where is the most exciting place you know?

______

8 Who is the most beautiful person you know?

______

Project

Design a Tourist Guide About Your Town

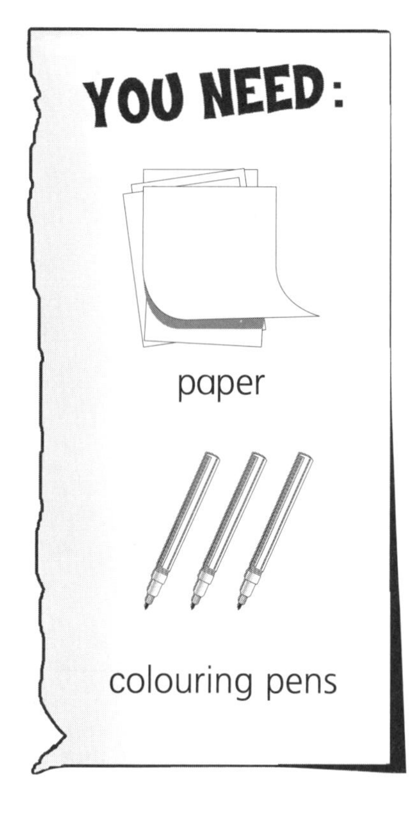

1 Write about where you live.

My Town

1. The hottest month is ______________ .
2. The coldest month is ______________ .
3. The busiest street is ______________ .
4. The largest shop is ______________ .
5. The most beautiful month is ______________ .
6. The largest building is ______________ .
7. The nicest place is ______________ .

2 Design a tourist guide about your town.

1. Fold the paper in 3.

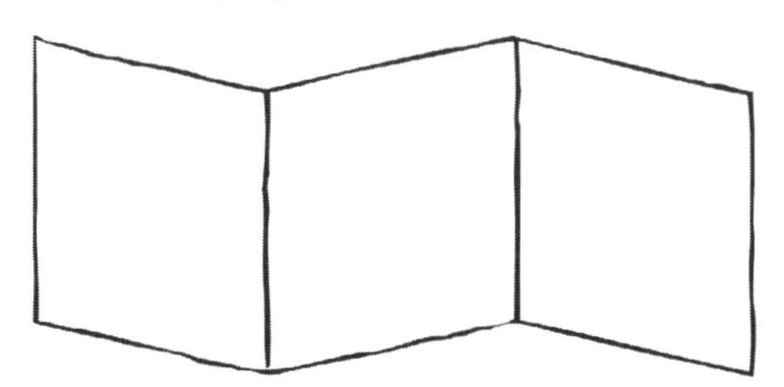

2. Design a cover.

3. Write about your town using information from Activity I.

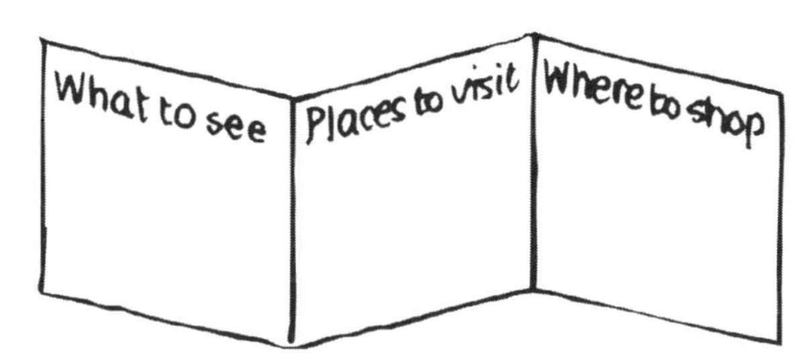

1 Match the sentences with a similar meaning.

1 It isn't clean enough. [f]
2 It isn't hot enough. [ ]
3 He isn't old enough. [ ]
4 He isn't fast enough. [ ]
5 They aren't rich enough. [ ]
6 It isn't loud enough. [ ]
7 She isn't tall enough. [ ]
8 She isn't brave enough. [ ]

a He's too young.
b They're too poor.
c She's too scared.
d She's too short.
e He's too slow.
f It's too dirty.
g It's too quiet.
h It's too cold.

2 Write the questions. Then write the answers using *too* and *enough*.

1 can't / fly / Why / a / plane? / you Why can't you fly a plane?

old | young Because I'm not old enough. I'm too young.

2 beach? / go / can't / we / Why / to / the ______

hot | cold Because it isn't ______

3 he / a / buy / can't / palace? / Why ______

rich | poor Because he isn't ______

4 mountain? / Why / the / you / can't / climb ______

safe | dangerous Because it isn't ______

1 Write. (What about you?)

What do you think?

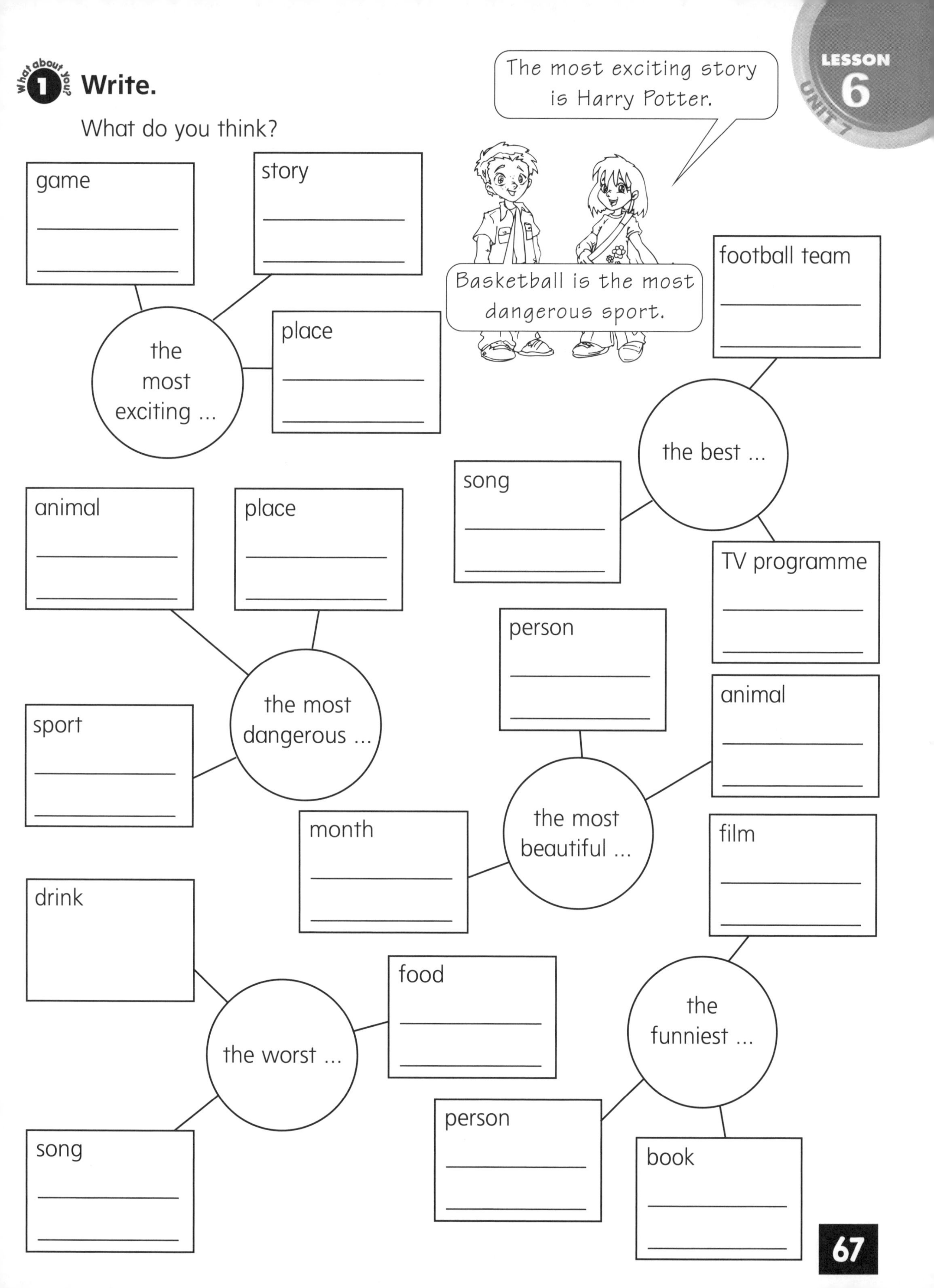

Phonics

1 Read.

One day Jim was thi**nk**i**ng** ...

2 Write *nk* or *ng* to match the words in the story.

1. ice-ri __ __
2. bri __ __
3. pi __ __
4. thi __ __ ing
5. si __ __
6. ju __ __ le
7. mo __ __ ey
8. so __ __
9. wi __ __ s

3 Write *true* or *false*.

1. Jim would like to sing a song. ____________
2. He'd like to bring a monkey to the toy shop. ____________
3. He'd like to be a king. ____________
4. He'd like to fly over the city. ____________

Try It!

LESSON 8
UNIT 7

1 Write sentences with a similar meaning.

1 They aren't old enough. They're too young.
2 He's too short. He isn't tall enough.
3 They aren't fast enough. ____________
4 She's too young. ____________
5 It's too loud. ____________
6 It isn't hot enough. ____________
7 He's too weak. ____________
8 She isn't quiet enough. ____________

2 Find the words. Then write the questions.

LOOK at your wordlist

1 drseeiifnlt f riendliest
2 euitbss b____________
3 ogtslne l____________
4 oehttst h____________
5 gisehht h____________

1 What / Who Who is the friendliest person in your class?
2 When / Where ____________ is the ____________ street in your town?
3 What / How ____________ is the ____________ river in your country?
4 Why / What ____________ is the ____________ month of the year?
5 Where / When ____________ is the ____________ mountain in your country?

The Challenge

1 Find the odd one out. Then write sentences.

1	oldest	smaller	fattest	longest
2	larger	busiest	luckiest	friendliest
3	faster	thinner	older	most beautiful
4	most famous	most expensive	most beautiful	better
5	louder	coldest	younger	richer
6	thinnest	saddest	more dangerous	fattest

1 ant / bird An ant is smaller than a bird.

2 elephant / horse ______

3 What / city / in the world? ______

4 Which / TV programme / 'The Simpsons'? ______

5 What / month / of the year? ______

6 crocodile / goat ______

What about you? **2 Write.**

1 Three things you're too young to do:

______ ______ ______

2 Three things you're too scared to do:

______ ______ ______

3 Three things that are larger than you:

______ ______ ______

4 Three things that are smaller than you:

______ ______ ______

3 Tick (✓) the words to complete Tara's message.

1	What's the largest animal?	an elephant	☐	My
		a camel	☐	His
2	What's the tallest animal?	a mouse	☐	dad
		a giraffe	☐	mum
3	Which city is hotter?	Cairo	☐	is
		London	☐	works
4	Where do elephants live?	England	☐	in
		Africa	☐	a
5	More than 20 million people live in Mexico City.	true	☐	police officer.
		false	☐	a restaurant.

Collect the correct words.

________ ________ ________ ________

________ ________

Does your mum work?

4 Make word crosses.

1

Down: d i r t i e _ t

Across: r u b b i s h ■ b i n

Across: _ t r e e t

2

Down: r e _ t a u r a n t

Across: b e _ t

3

Down: f r i e n d l _ e s t

Across: a n _ m a l

Now write sentences using each word cross.

1 ______________________________

2 ______________________________

3 ______________________________

LESSON 1 UNIT 8

Helping Hands

1 Look and match.

a  • sweep the floor

b  • do the laundry

c  • do the ironing

d  • do the washing-up

e  • feed the dog

f  • water the plants

g  • make the bed

h  • clean the windows

2 Look at the pictures and say what they did yesterday.

a Yesterday he did the ironing.

b ______________________________

c ______________________________

d ______________________________

e ______________________________

f ______________________________

g ______________________________

h ______________________________

1 Look and write.

He She It	has got to	go to bed. go to school. buy a new book. write a letter. get the bus.
I You We They	have got to	

1 I have got to get the bus.

2 ______________________________

3 ______________________________

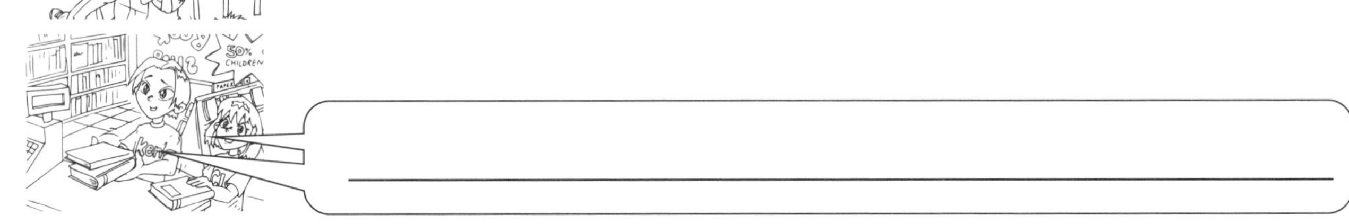

4 ______________________________

5 ______________________________

What about you? 2 Write three things that you have got to do today.

I have got to ______________________________

____

______________________________.

LESSON 3 UNIT 8

1 Write and choose *true* or *false*.

+ = We have got to	− = We haven't got to

At school:

1 speak English + We have got to speak English. (true) / false

2 cook − ______ true / false

3 play games + ______ true / false

4 sing songs + ______ true / false

5 listen to our teacher − ______ true / false

6 clean the windows + ______ true / false

7 eat sweets − ______ true / false

8 write in our notebooks + ______ true / false

What about you? 2 Write using *I have got to* or *I haven't got to*.

1 ______ go to school.

2 ______ do the laundry.

3 ______ do my homework.

4 ______ make my bed.

5 ______ sweep the floor.

6 ______ pick up my clothes.

7 ______ do the washing-up.

8 ______ walk to school.

9 ______ clean the windows.

What are your three most important rules?

1 I have got to ______

2 ______

3 ______

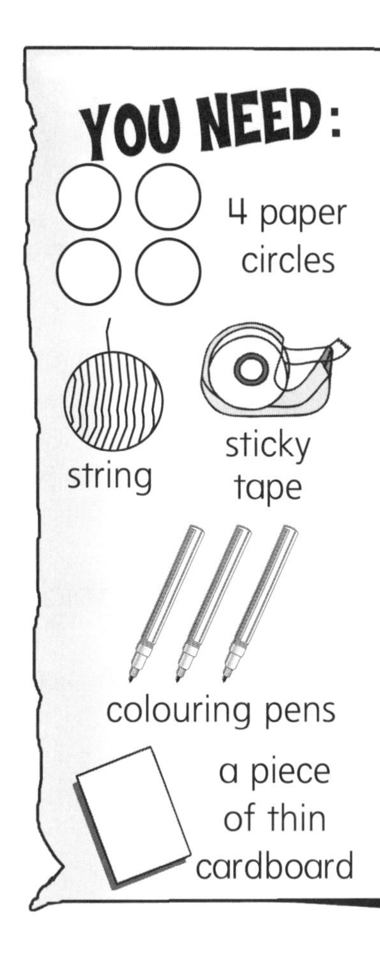

1 Make a class display.

1 Draw pictures and write things you have got to do on the circles.

2 Write your name on the cardboard.

3 Use sticky tape to fix your work onto the string.

4 Hang up your display.

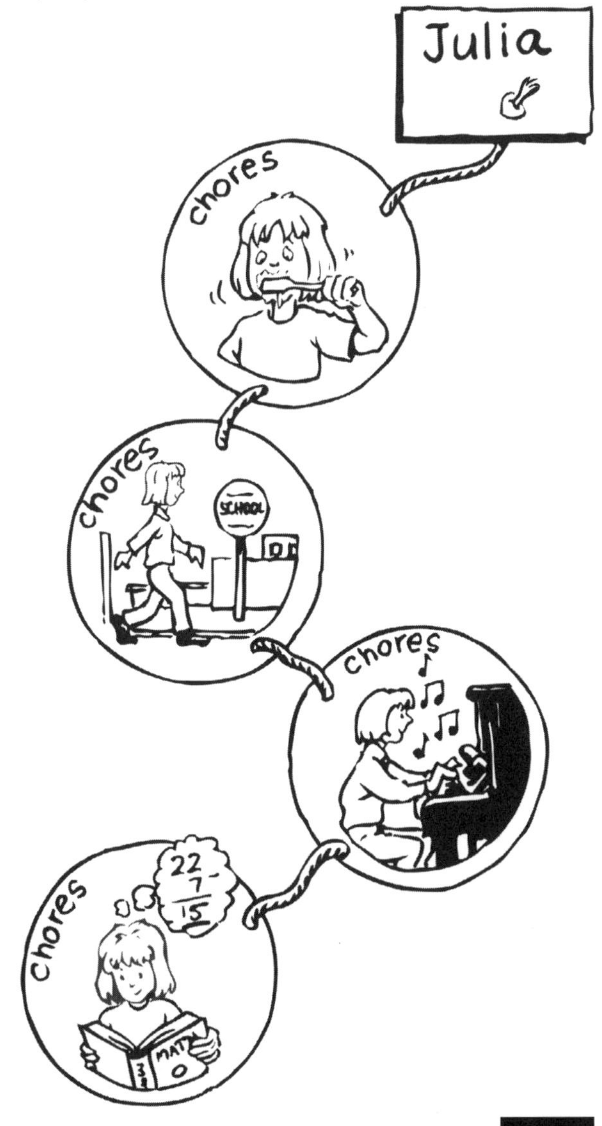

2 Look at the display.

Can you find someone who ...

1 ... has got to do their homework?

____

2 ... has got to study science?

____

3 ... has got to share a bedroom?

____

4 ... has got to clean their bedroom?

____

5 ... has got to do the washing-up?

____

6 ... has got to practise the piano?

____

LESSON 5 UNIT 8

1 Complete the questions. Then choose and write the correct answers.

go buy study wait ~~run~~ listen do ~~hit~~ look for take

1 I want to play tennis. What have I got to do? — You have got to run _____ fast. You have got to hit _____ the ball.

2 I want to go to Japan. __________ — __________ a ticket. __________ the plane.

3 We want to study English. __________ — __________ to school. __________ to your teacher.

4 They want to do well in their exams. __________ — __________ hard. __________ their homework.

5 They want to cross the street. __________ — __________ on the pavement. __________ cars.

2 Answer.

What about you?

1 What time have you got to get up on school days? __________

2 What time have you got to go to bed? __________

3 When have you got to do your homework? __________

4 Why have you got to eat your vegetables? __________

5 Where have you got to go when you're ill? __________

6 Who have you got to listen to at school? __________

1 Complete the questions. Then write true answers.

What has your best friend got to do?

1 Has he/she got to ______ get up early? ______
2 ______ go to bed early? ______
3 ______ take the bus to school? ______
4 ______ share a bedroom? ______
5 ______ help out at home? ______
6 ______ study geography? ______

2 Guess then ask a friend.

Has your friend got to ...

1 ... take out the rubbish? yes / no ______
2 ... do the washing-up? yes / no ______
3 ... clean his / her bedroom? yes / no ______
4 ... make his / her bed? yes / no ______
5 ... feed a pet? yes / no ______
6 ... help do the laundry? yes / no ______
7 ... help do the shopping? yes / no ______
8 ... get up early on Sundays? yes / no ______
9 ... do his / her homework on Saturdays? yes / no ______
10 ... make breakfast? yes / no ______

3 Check with your friend.

Were your guesses correct? Give yourself one point for each correct guess.

9–10	6–8	0–5
Congratulations! You're the best friend. You know everything.	Pretty good. But you could find out more about your best friend.	Find out more about your best friend. They need you!

Phonics

1 Read.

Katy wa**nt**ed to go camping. She walked to the po**nd** and put up her te**nt**.

But she fou**nd** some a**nt**s in her te**nt** so she se**nt** them away.

Then she fou**nd** some a**nt**s on her ha**nd**s so she se**nt** them away.

A**nd** then she had a**nt**s in her sa**nd**als! So Katy ran away.

2 Write *nd* or *nt* to match the words in the story.

1 a __ __ s
2 wa __ __ ed
3 wa __ __
4 fou __ __
5 ha __ __ s
6 po __ __
7 te __ __
8 sa __ __ als
9 se __ __

3 Look at the story and number the sentences.

1 And then she had ants in her sandals! ☐
2 'I don't want ants in my tent.' ☐
3 She walked to the pond and put up her tent. ☐
4 'I don't want ants on my hands.' ☐

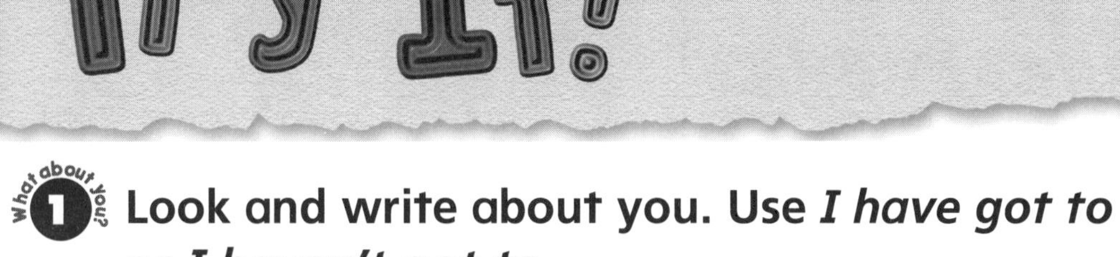

LOOK at your wordlist

1 Look and write about you. Use *I have got to* or *I haven't got to*.

1 I have got to do the washing-up. ______

2 ______

3 ______

4 ______

5 ______

2 Write the opposites.

1 He has got to study English. ______

2 She has got to sweep the floor. ______

3 Dad has got to do the ironing. ______

4 My brother has got to clean his bedroom. ______

5 He hasn't got to cook dinner. ______

6 She hasn't got to do her homework. ______

7 They haven't got to walk to school. ______

8 Mum hasn't got to do the laundry. ______

The Challenge

1 **Complete the charts.**

~~drink~~	wash	brush their hair	close their eyes	run	go to school
eat	read	study	sleep	go shopping	get up early
write	listen	brush their teeth	wear clothes		

Children have got to ...	
______	______
______	______
______	______
______	______

Children and animals have got to ...	
drink	______
______	______
______	______
______	______

2 **Write.**

In your house ...

1 Who has got to clean the windows? ______

2 Who has got to cook? ______

3 Who has got to sweep the floor? ______

4 Who has got to do the washing-up? ______

5 Who has got to do the ironing? ______

6 Who has got to do the laundry? ______

7 Who has got to clean your bedroom? ______

8 Who has got to make your bed? ______

How many of these things has your mum got to do? ☐

How many of these things have you got to do? ☐

3 Tick (✓) the words to complete Tara's message.

1	Where have people got to wait?	at a bus stop	☐	Dolphins
		at a lamp post	☐	Cats
2	Where have children got to study?	at an ice-rink	☐	eat
		at school	☐	have got to
3	What have you got to do every day?	eat	☐	live
		fly	☐	fish
4	What have you got to do every night?	sleep	☐	in the
		disappear	☐	and
5	What have cows got to eat?	sweets	☐	meat.
		grass	☐	sea.

Collect the correct words.

_______ _______ ___ _______ ___ ___ _________

What other animals live in the sea?

4 What comes next?

1 enoughtootooenoughtootooenoughtootooenoughtooenoughtoo ____________.

2 windowfloorfloorfloorwindowfloorfloorfloorwindowfloorfloor ____________.

3 hashavetohashavetohashavetohashavetohashavetohashaveto ____________.

4 waterwashwashwaterwashwashwaterwashwashwaterwash ____________.

5 plantsdishesplantsdishesplantsdishesplantsdishesplantsdishes ____________.

LESSON 1 UNIT

9 Around the World

1 Find the countries. Then write the names.

I	N	D	A	I	N	I	**I**	N	D	I	A
G	**E**	N	G	L	A	N	D	N	L	A	E
S	O	U	T	H	K	O	R	E	A	S	K
G	T	P	E	Y	**E**	G	Y	P	T	G	P
X	C	O	**M**	E	X	I	C	O	M	E	X
I	B	A	Z	R	**B**	R	A	Z	I	L	L
S	T	R	**A**	U	S	T	R	A	L	I	A
U	**T**	H	E	U	S	A	H	E	U	T	A

1 India
2 ____________
3 ____________
4 ____________
5 ____________
6 ____________
7 ____________
8 ____________

2 Label the map with the countries.

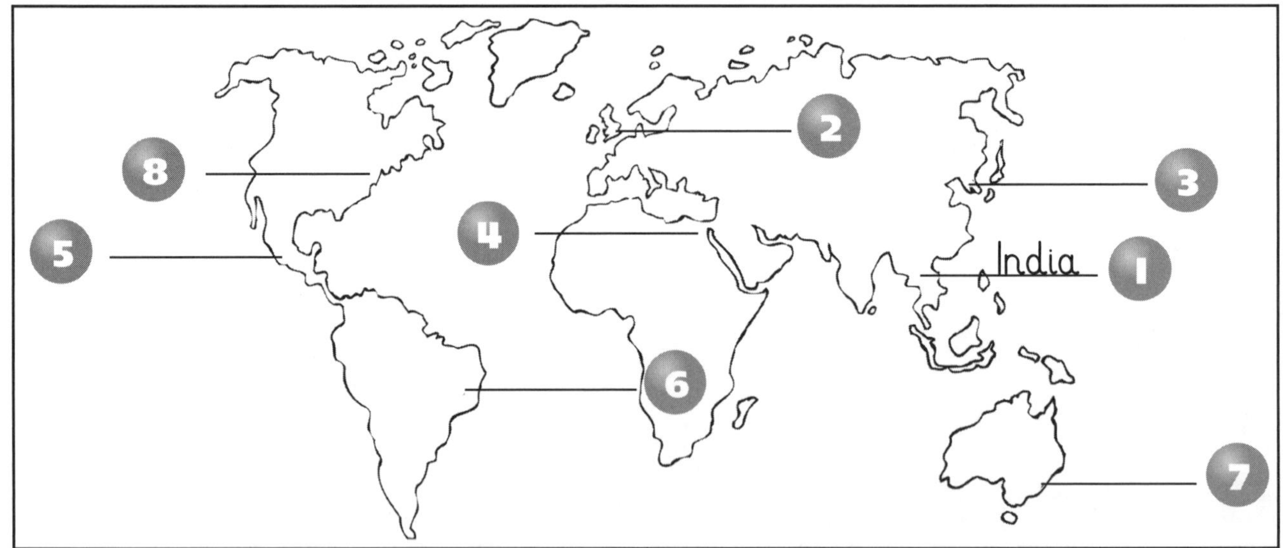

3 Write.

1 Mumbai is in India.
2 London is in ____________.
3 Seoul is in ____________.
4 Cairo is in ____________.
5 Acapulco is in ____________.
6 Rio de Janeiro is in ____________.
7 Sydney is in ____________.
8 New York is in ____________.

1 Look at picture A then picture B and tick (✓) the true sentences. Then write the secret word.

In picture B ...

1	The cat has disappeared.	✓	f
2	The cat is sitting in a tree.		w
3	The man has cleaned his car.		i
4	The man is cleaning his car.		m
5	The boy has painted a picture.		s
6	The boy is painting a picture.		a
7	The girl has turned around.		h
8	The girl is looking at the flowers.		p

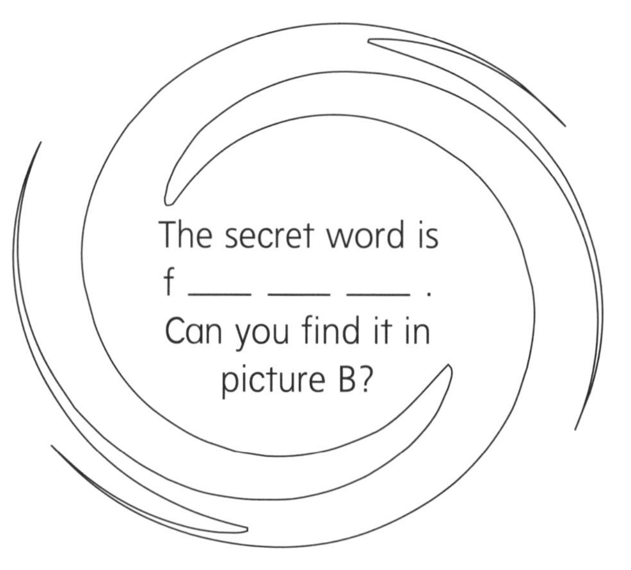

2 Write the short form of the sentences.

1 She has disappeared. She's disappeared.

2 I have finished my homework. ______________________

3 They have followed Stig. ______________________

4 We have noticed the picture. ______________________

5 He has climbed a mountain. ______________________

6 She has played basketball. ______________________

1 Match the opposites.

1 He's climbed a mountain. [f]
2 She hasn't cleaned her room. [ ]
3 They've walked up a hill. [ ]
4 She's watched a film. [ ]
5 They've danced on a beach. [ ]
6 He's travelled through the USA. [ ]
7 They haven't finished their homework. [ ]
8 He hasn't played basketball. [ ]

a She's cleaned her room.
b They haven't danced on a beach.
c He's played basketball.
d They've finished their homework.
e They haven't walked up a hill.
f He hasn't climbed a mountain.
g He hasn't travelled through the USA.
h She hasn't watched a film.

2 Write the opposites.

1 They haven't finished. They've finished.
2 She's washed her hair. ______
3 He's taken the bus. ______
4 I haven't repaired my computer. ______
5 He's painted a picture. ______
6 She's done the washing-up. ______
7 They haven't visited England. ______
8 It's climbed a tree. ______
9 They haven't watched this film. ______
10 He's listened to this song. ______

1 Choose a country.

This is a project about ______________________ .

2 Choose and colour a map.

Egypt

Mexico

India

the USA

Brazil

3 Find out and write.

The capital city is ______________ .

A famous place to visit in ______________ is ______________ .

4 Find out and write.

A famous person from ______________________________ is ______________________________ .

5 Tick (✔) all the things you can find in this country.

beaches ☐

mountains ☐

deserts ☐

cities ☐

6 Find out and write.

A traditional food: ______________

A popular sport: ______________

An animal: ______________

1 Complete the questions. Then look and answer.

1 Has she brushed her teeth today? ________

2 ________ he played football today? ________

3 ________ they walked in the mountains today? ________

4 ________ they painted a picture today? ________

5 ________ she danced today? ________

2 Answer the questions.

What about you?

What have you done today?

1 Have you brushed your hair? ________

2 Have you brushed your teeth? ________

3 Have you called a friend? ________

4 Have you walked to the shops? ________

5 Have you played a game? ________

6 Have you used a computer? ________

7 Have you danced? ________

3 Look at Activity 2. Then write.

What about you?

Today I've ________

________.

1 Read and circle.

How many of these things have you done in your life?

How many countries have you visited?
0 / 1–3 / more than 3

How many hotels have you stayed in?
0 / 1–3 / more than 3

How many times have you played on the beach?
0 / 1–3 / more than 3

How many times have you played the piano?
0 / 1–3 / more than 3

How many museums have you visited?
0 / 1–3 / more than 3

How many times have you travelled by train?
0 / 1–3 / more than 3

How many cities have you visited?
0 / 1–3 / more than 3

How many mountains have you climbed?
0 / 1–3 / more than 3

2 Write your answers to Activity 1.

1 I've visited ______ countries.

2 I've ______ hotels.

3 I've ______ museums.

4 I've ______ on the beach ______ times.

5 I've ______ the piano ______ times.

6 I've ______ by train ______ times.

7 I've ______ cities.

8 I've ______ mountains.

Phonics

1 Read.

Smudge is a **sm**all, clever cat. Today it's **sn**owing so **Sm**udge has stayed at home. She's **sm**iling.

She's **sm**ashed a vase with her tail.

She's played with a **sn**orkel.

She's played with a **sn**ake. Now she's not **sm**iling!

2 Write *sm* or *sn* to match the words in the story.

1 __ __ all
2 __ __ udge
3 __ __ ashed
4 __ __ owing
5 __ __ ake
6 __ __ iling
7 __ __ orkel

3 Look at the story and complete the sentences.

1 She's a small, clever cat. She's ______________________ .

2 It's ______________ so ______________ has stayed at home.

3 She's ______________ a ______________ with her tail.

4 She's played ______________________ .

Try It!

LESSON 8 UNIT 9

1 Write using *I've* or *I haven't*.

What about you?

What have you done today?

1 (do) the washing-up ______________________

2 (clean) my trainers ______________________

3 (brush) my teeth ______________________

4 (play) a game ______________________

5 (walk) to school ______________________

6 (watch) TV ______________________

2 Find and write the countries in alphabetical order.

LOOK at your wordlist

OMIXEC	RLIABZ	IURTSAALA
M______	B______	A______

UHTOS	RAEOK	ADNII
S______	K______	I______

NDAGNEL	TPGEY	EHT	SUA
E______	E______	T______	U______

1 ______________ 4 ______________ 7 ______________

2 ______________ 5 ______________ 8 ______________

3 ______________ 6 ______________

The Challenge

1 Look and label the sentences.

Today ...

1 He's climbed a tree. ☐

2 She's walked to school. ☐

3 They've played tennis. ☐

4 She's done the washing-up. ☐

5 He's helped his mum. ☐

6 They've repaired a bowl. ☐

2 Write.

1 Two things you have got to do every day.

I have got to brush my teeth. ______ I have got to wash my face. ______

2 Two things you have got to do at school.

______ ______

3 Two things you have done today.

______ ______

4 Two things you haven't done today.

______ ______

3 Tick (✓) the words to complete Tara's message.

1	Which country is larger?	Australia	☐	My
		England	☐	I'd
2	Which country is smaller?	the USA	☐	like
		South Korea	☐	best
3	Which country is hotter?	Mexico	☐	holiday
		England	☐	to
4	Which country is wetter?	Colombia	☐	was in
		Egypt	☐	visit
5	Which country has the most famous football team?	India	☐	Mexico.
		Brazil	☐	the Caribbean.

Collect the correct words.

____ ____ ____________ ____ ____ ____ __________

Where was yours?

4 Look and tick (✓). Then write.

1

I've played ...	
football	☐
tennis	☐
golf	☐
volleyball	☐

2

PARK

I've walked to ...	
the shops	☐
the park	☐
the ice-rink	☐
school	☐

3

BRAZIL

I've visited ...	
a museum	☐
a safari park	☐
India	☐
Brazil	☐

1 ______________________________

2 ______________________________

3 ______________________________

LESSON 1 UNIT

10 Nature

1 Complete the pictures. Then write.

stream	palm tree	waterfall	sand	cave	coconut	cactus	leaves

1 
____

2 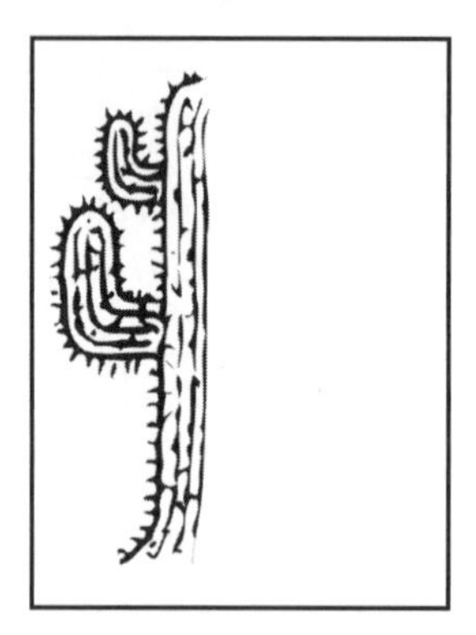
____

3 
____

4 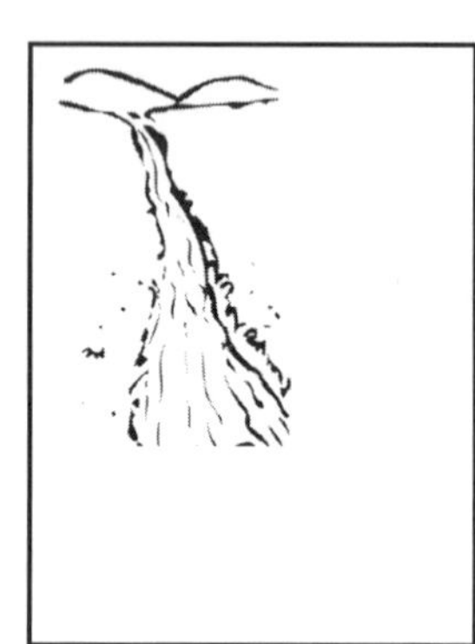
____

5 
____

6 
____

7 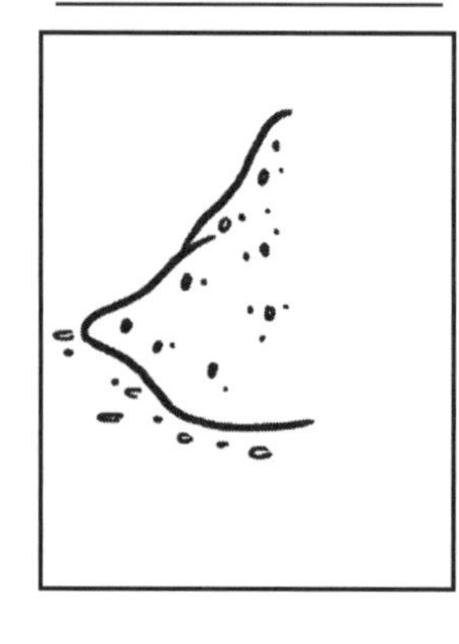
____

8 
____

What about you? 2 Answer the questions.

1 Is there a cave near your house? ______________

2 Are the leaves green on the trees? ______________

3 Is there a waterfall near your town? ______________

4 Is there a stream near your house? ______________

5 Do you like eating coconuts? ______________

6 Is a palm tree taller than a cactus? ______________

7 Do you like playing in the sand? ______________

1 **Colour the present tense verbs yellow. Colour the present perfect tense verbs blue.**

have ridden	sleep	see	have drunk	eat	have had
lose	fall	have swum	ride	have lost	swim
have eaten	have seen	drink	have fallen	have	have slept

2 **Complete the chart.**

Present	see	eat	swim	have	ride	drink	sleep
Past simple	saw	ate	______	had	______	drank	______
Present perfect	have seen	have ______	have swum	have ______	have ridden	have ______	have slept

3 **Match.**

	Present	**Past**	**Present perfect**
1	swim	lost	have eaten
2	ride	saw	have slept
3	have	drank	have lost
4	see	swam	have had
5	sleep	slept	have ridden
6	lose	ate	have drunk
7	eat	rode	have swum
8	drink	had	have seen

LESSON 3 UNIT 10

1 Count the syllables. Then write.

1	ridden	2	5	eaten	____	9	fallen	____
2	swum	____	6	coconut	____	10	camel	____
3	found	____	7	kangaroo	____	11	lake	____
4	ever	____	8	king	____	12	ladybird	____

Words with one syllable: ____________ ____________ ____________ ____________

Words with two syllables: ____________ ____________ ____________ ____________ ____________

Words with three syllables: ____________ ____________ ____________

2 What about you? Answer using *Yes, I have* or *No, I haven't*.

1 Have you ever met a film star? ____________________

2 Have you ever made a cake? ____________________

3 Have you ever seen a ladybird? ____________________

4 Have you ever found a bracelet? ____________________

5 Have you ever eaten octopus? ____________________

6 Have you ever ridden a camel? ____________________

7 Have you ever swum in a lake? ____________________

8 Have you ever slept on a mountain? ____________________

1 **Answer the questions.**

1 Are there deserts in your country?

____

2 Are deserts hot or cold during the day?

____

3 Are they hot or cold at night?

____

4 Are they wet or dry places?

____

5 What plants do you find in a desert?

____

6 What animals do you see in a desert?

____

2 **Cut out pictures from magazines.**

3 **Make a picture of a desert. Add labels.**

1 Write the sentences using *ago*. Then number the timeline.

1 He's been friends with Charles for ten years.

2 He's worked in a restaurant for two years.

3 He's lived in the city for seven years.

4 He hasn't called Charles for two weeks.

5 He's been ill since last Sunday.

1 He met Charles ten years ago.

2 He started ______

3 He moved ______

4 He called ______

5 He became ______

1				
ten years ago	seven years ago	two years ago	two weeks ago	last Sunday

2 Complete the sentences about you.

1 I've had a ______ since ______ .

2 I've had a ______ for ______ .

3 I've liked ______ since ______ .

4 I've liked ______ for ______ .

5 I've played ______ since ______ .

6 I've played ______ for ______ .

7 I've lived in ______ since ______ .

8 I've lived in ______ for ______ .

1 Write about your favourite things. Then answer the questions.

What about you?

My favourite toy ______________

My least favourite toy ______________

My favourite clothes ______________

My least favourite clothes ______________

My favourite food ______________

My least favourite food ______________

1 How long have you had your favourite clothes?
Since ____ .

2 How long have you liked your favourite food?
For ____ .

3 How long have you liked your favourite toy?
Since ____ .

4 When was the last time you wore your least favourite clothes?
____ ago.

5 How long have you disliked your least favourite toy?
Since ____ .

6 When was the last time you ate your least favourite food?
____ ago.

2 Choose and write.

Who would you ask these questions?

a farmer	a lifeguard	a king	a musician

1 How long have you lived in a palace? ______________

2 How long have you had this barn? ______________

3 How long have you played the piano? ______________

4 How long have you worked at the beach? ______________

Phonics

1 Read.

Have you ever had a **sp**ider on your **sp**oon?

Have you ever read a **st**ory about a **st**atue?

Have you ever heard a **st**arfish **sp**eak?

Have you ever walked along a **st**range **st**reet on a **st**ormy night?

2 Write *sp* or *st* to match the words in the story.

1 __ __ oon
2 __ __ arfish
3 __ __ range
4 __ __ ormy
5 __ __ eak
6 __ __ atue
7 __ __ ider
8 __ __ reet
9 __ __ aring
10 __ __ ory

3 Look at the story and complete the questions.

1 Have you ever heard ______________________________?
2 Have you ever walked ______________________________?
3 Have you ever had ______________________________?
4 Have you ever read ______________________________?

Try It!

LESSON 8 UNIT 10

1 **Write the verbs in the present perfect.**

LOOK at your wordlist

1 have (be)
2 have (eat)
3 have (lose)
4 have (swim)
5 have (make)
6 have (sleep)
7 have (see)
8 have (have)
9 have (meet)

2 **Complete the sentences.**

waterfall	sand	cactus	leaves	palm tree	stream	cave	coconuts

1 The desert is usually made of ______________ .

2 They went over the bridge to cross the ______________ .

3 There were green ______________ on the tree.

4 There were ______________ growing on the ______________ ______________ .

5 A ______________ is usually found in the desert.

6 They walked inside the ______________ and found treasure.

7 There was water falling 100 metres at the ______________ .

The Challenge

1 **Read and write using *Yesterday* or *Today*.**

1 Today I've eaten an apple.

2 ______________ I went to the city.

3 ______________ he's made some ice cream.

4 ______________ he stayed in a hotel.

5 ______________ she's lost her watch.

6 ______________ she's sent an e-mail.

7 ______________ he's painted a picture.

8 ______________ they travelled by train.

9 ______________ he's spoken to his teacher.

What about you? **2** **Answer the questions.**

1 How long have you been a student at this school?

____

2 How long have you been in school today?

____

3 When did you start learning English?

____

4 Have you ever been to England?

____

3 Tick (✓) the words to complete Tara's message.

Collect the correct words.

1	Shells are usually	on the pavement.	☐	Do
		on the beach.	☐	I've
2	Caves are usually	dark.	☐	drunk
		light.	☐	you
3	A cactus usually has	horns.	☐	like
		spikes.	☐	three
4	A waterfall is usually	loud.	☐	colas
		quiet.	☐	dark
5	Coconuts are usually	hard.	☐	today.
		soft.	☐	caves.

_______ _______ _______ _______ _______

How many have you had?

4 Complete the word crosses.

1

			f	
			o	
			l	
	I		l	
	n		o	
	d		w	
t		g		r
	a		d	

2

			v		
			i		
			s		
			i		
			t		
m	u	s		u	m
			d		

3

r	e	p	a	i		e	d
					i		
					n		
					g		

Now write sentences using *I've* or *I haven't*.

1 ______________________________

2 ______________________________

3 ______________________________

LESSON 1 UNIT 11

Work

1 Find and write.

scientist	magician	house painter	builder	vet	farmer
cleaner	photographer	teacher	doctor		

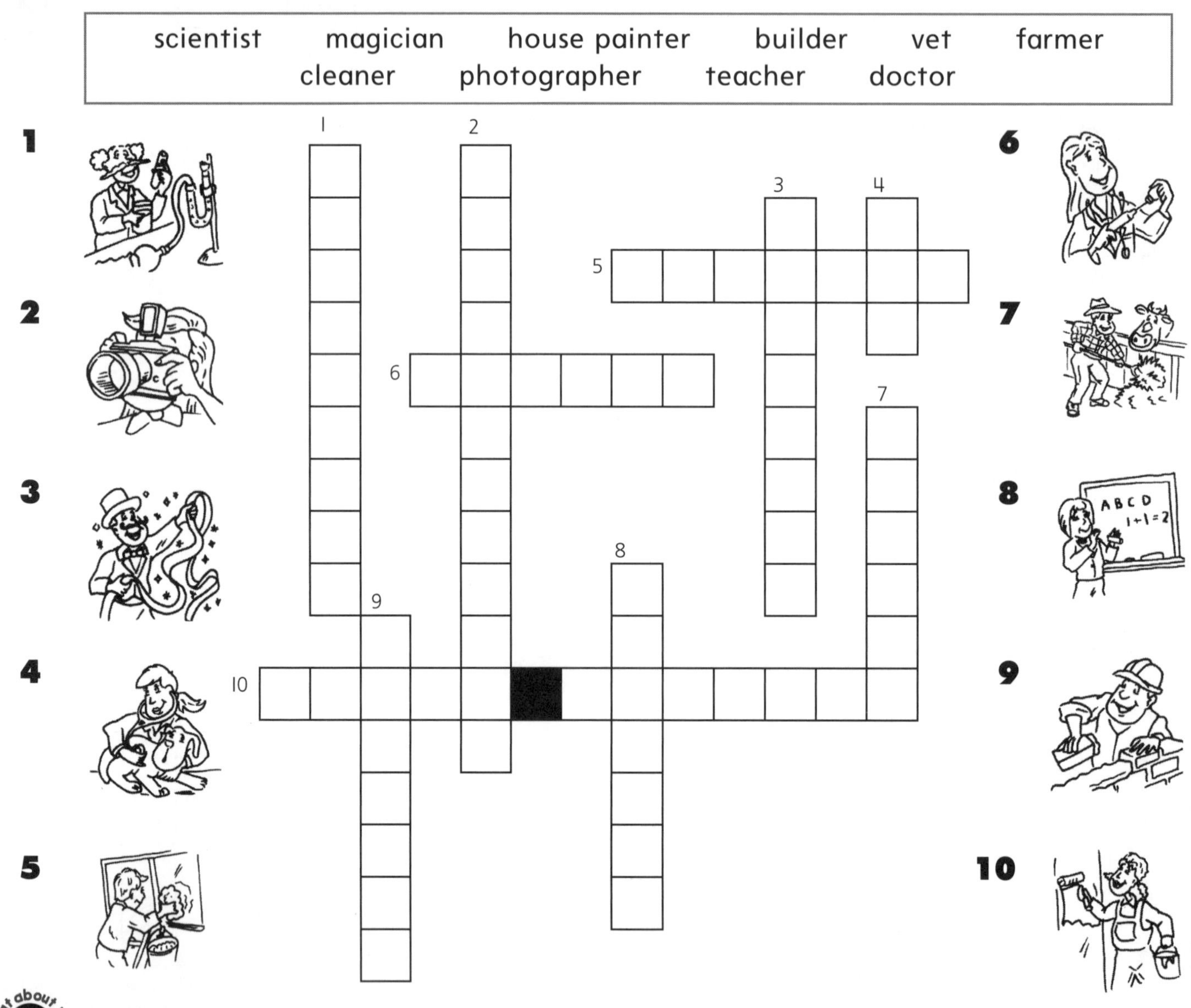

2 Write.

What about you?

Do you know ...

1 ... the name of a doctor? ______________________

2 ... the name of a teacher? ______________________

3 ... the name of a photographer? ______________________

4 ... the name of a builder? ______________________

1 Write. Then match to the pictures.

a car	a cleaner	~~a photographer~~	a music teacher	
a turtle	a motorcycle	a sheep	a vet	an aeroplane

1 A person who takes photographs. a photographer [e]

2 A machine that flies. ______ [ ]

3 A machine that has two wheels. ______ [ ]

4 An animal that eats grass. ______ [ ]

5 A person who teaches music. ______ [ ]

6 An animal that lives in the sea. ______ [ ]

7 A person who takes care of sick animals. ______ [ ]

8 A machine that has four wheels. ______ [ ]

9 A person who cleans houses. ______ [ ]

a b c d e f g h i

2 Find and write.

Find a person ...

1 ... who likes reading. Sophie is a person who likes reading.

2 ... who has helped a sick animal. ______

3 ... who has been to the USA. ______

4 ... who has seen a dinosaur fossil. ______

5 ... who likes playing football. ______

6 ... who has been to a cave. ______

7 ... who has seen a giraffe. ______

8 ... who likes painting. ______

LESSON 3 UNIT 11

1 Write the rhyming words.

knits classes talks
car mouse clocks
bear these

1 house ______
2 sits ______
3 wear ______
4 glasses ______
5 trees ______
6 walks ______
7 socks ______
8 are ______

2 Match and write.

the bedroom the park the sea ~~school~~
the dining room the bathroom

1 A place where you study English. school

2 A place where you eat dinner. ______

3 A place where you ride your bike. ______

4 A place where you sleep. ______

5 A place where you go swimming. ______

6 A place where you wash. ______

1 School is a place where I study English.
2 ______
3 ______
4 ______
5 ______
6 ______

LOOK at your wordlist

What about you? **1** **Complete the chart.**

MY TOP FIVE INVENTIONS		
	Invention	It's a machine that ...
1st		
2nd		
3rd		
4th		
5th		

2 **Design your own robot.**

Think about: what the robot does
what it looks like
why it is important

3 **Draw your robot.**

4 **Label any important parts.**

5 **Write about your robot.**

This is a robot that ______________________________
______________________________.
It has got ______________________________
______________________________.
It can ______________________________
______________________________.

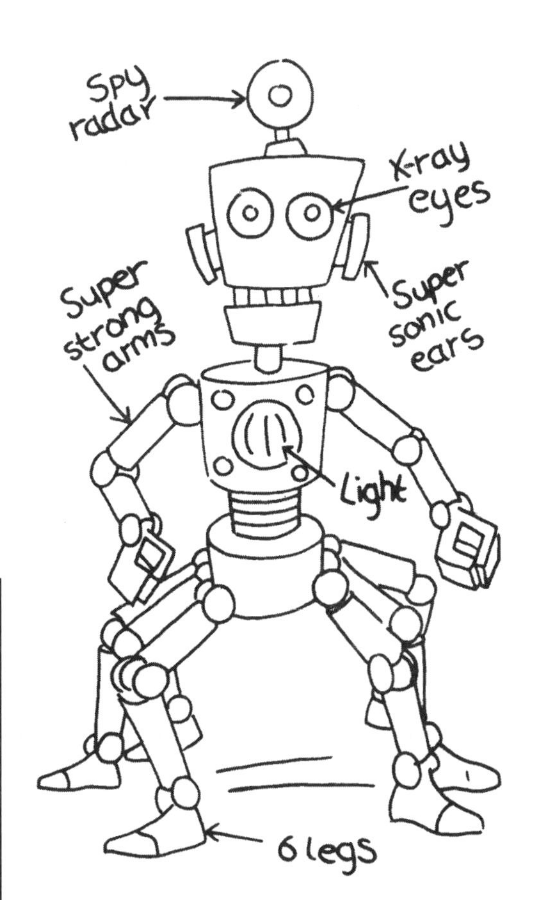

LESSON 5 UNIT 11

1 Complete the sentences using *where, that* or *who*. Then number the pictures.

1 This is the place ________ they used to go to school.

2 This is the car ________ he used to drive.

3 This is the cinema ________ they used to go.

4 This is the beach ________ they used to swim.

5 This is the barn ________ the cows used to live.

6 This is the cleaner ________ used to clean our house.

What about you? 2 Choose one from each section and tick (✔). Then draw and write.

This is the bed that I used to sleep in.

where		that	
school / study	☐	computer / have	☐
zoo / visit	☐	doll / play with	☐
shop / buy CDs	☐	bed / sleep in	✔
park / play frisbee	☐	bus / take	☐

1 ____________________

____

2 ____________________

____

1 Solve the puzzle.

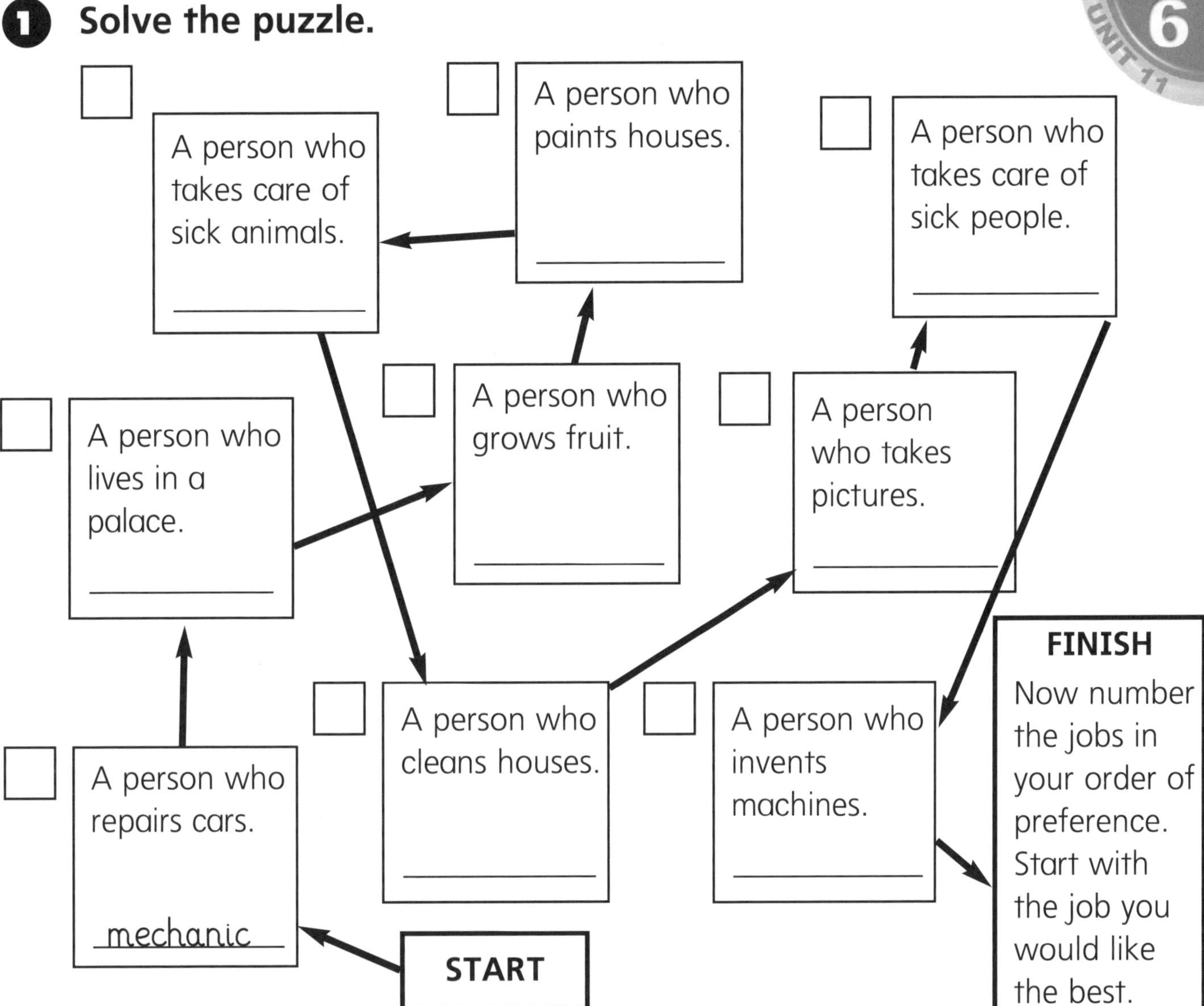

2 Write about two adults you know.

Think about these things:
Who is it?
What does he / she do?
How long has he / she done this job?
Where does he / she work?
What time does he / she start work?
Does he / she have to speak English at work?

Person 1: ______________________

____

____

____

Person 2: ______________________

____

____

____

LESSON 7 UNIT 11

Phonics

1 Read.

He can **sk**i on the smallest **sk**is.
He's Super**sk**unk!

He can **sw**im the deepest river.
He's Super**sk**unk!

He can **sw**ing from the tallest trees.
He's Super**sk**unk!

But he doesn't smell **sw**eet.
He's Super**sk**unk!

2 Write *sk* or *sw* to match the words in the story.

1 Super __ __ unk
2 __ __ i
3 __ __ eet
4 __ __ ing
5 __ __ is
6 __ __ im

3 Write *true* or *false*.

1 Superskunk can ski. ____________
2 Superskunk can swim. ____________
3 Superskunk can swing from the trees. ____________
4 Superskunk smells sweet. ____________

Try It!

LESSON 8 UNIT 11

1 Tick (✓) the true sentences.

1
This is a person who builds houses. ☐
This is a person who grows fruit. ☐

2
This is a machine that takes pictures. ☐
This is a machine that plays films. ☐

3
This is a machine that cleans the floor. ☐
This is a machine that makes clothes. ☐

4
This is a person who plays football. ☐
This is a person who plays music. ☐

2 Choose. Then complete the sentences using *where*, *that* or *who*.

eat	takes	comes	~~watch~~	swim

1 A cinema is a place <u>where</u> you can <u>watch</u> films.

2 A photographer is a person ________ ________ pictures.

3 A restaurant is a place ________ you can ________ .

4 An elephant is an animal ________ ________ from India.

5 The beach is a place ________ you can ________ .

The Challenge

1 Find the odd one out. Then write sentences.

1	who	(photographer)	how	why
2	TV	drive	sleep	have
3	been	done	seen	teacher
4	spoken	grown	bedroom	ridden
5	scientist	clock	builder	doctor
6	cinema	India	Egypt	Mexico

1 person / takes pictures A photographer is a person who takes pictures.

2 machine / we watch ______

3 person / teaches English ______

4 place / we sleep ______

5 machine / tells the time ______

6 place / we go to watch films ______

2 Find the question. Then write your answer.

[palm tree] = vet [cactus] = you [leaves] = Do [waterfall] = a [coconut] = know

leaves cactus coconut waterfall palm tree

Question: ______ ______ ______ ______ ______ ?

Your answer: ______

3 Tick (✓) the words to complete Tara's message.

Collect the correct words.

1	It's a place where you can eat.	a restaurant	☐	I'd
		a mountain	☐	He's
2	It's a place where you usually sleep.	a bedroom	☐	like
		school	☐	talked
3	It's a person who usually works outside.	a music teacher	☐	to
		a builder	☐	to be
4	It's a person who usually works with animals.	a house painter	☐	a
		a vet	☐	an
5	It's a person who usually works in a school.	a teacher	☐	inventor.
		a photographer	☐	magician.

_____ _________ ____ ____ ____ __________

What would you like to be?

4 What comes next?

1 vetvetbuilderdoctorvetvetbuilderdoctorvetvetbuilder ____________ .

2 IndiaIndiaBrazilBrazilIndiaIndiaBrazilBrazilIndiaIndiaBrazil ____________ .

3 housepaintermagicianmagicianhousepaintermagician ____________ .

4 leavesleavesleavespalmtreeleavesleavesleavespalmtreeleavesleaves ____________ .

5 citycountrycitycountrycitycountrycitycountrycitycountrycity ____________ .

LESSON 1 UNIT 12

The Carnival

1 Find and write the labels.

1 
hot dog

2 
candyfloss

3 
acrobat

4 
fire-eater

5 
float

6 
dancer

7 
juggler

8 
clown

2 Look at Activity I. Then complete the chart.

5 letters
____
____

6 letters
dancer
______ ______

7 letters
____
____

9 letters
____

10 letters
____

What about you? 1 Write about the things you will do after school today.

something that I'll eat	something that I'll do	something that I'll watch on TV	something that I'll read	something that I'll drink
______	______	______	______	______
______	______	______	______	______
______	______	______	______	______

What about you? 2 Choose and tick (✓) six activities. Then write.

What will you do during the holidays?

1 I'll ______
2 ______
3 ______
4 ______
5 ______
6 ______

- swim in the sea ☐
- visit a museum ☐
- play on my computer ☐
- visit a zoo ☐
- go to a carnival ☐
- go to the mountains ☐
- visit my cousins ☐
- ride my bike ☐
- go to the USA ☐
- speak English ☐

What about you? 3 Write four sentences about what you will do this weekend.

1 go I'll go ______
2 visit ______
3 play ______
4 eat ______

LESSON 3 UNIT 12

1 Count the syllables and write.

1 won't __1__ 4 never ____ 7 clarinet ____

2 beautiful ____ 5 will ____ 8 dancer ____

3 children ____ 6 acrobat ____ 9 float ____

Words with one syllable: ____________ ____________ ____________

Words with two syllables: ____________ ____________ ____________

Words with three syllables: ____________ ____________ ____________

What about you? 2 Complete the questions. Then answer using *Yes, I will* or *No, I won't*.

What will you do tomorrow?

1 __Will__ you read a magazine? ____________________

2 ______ you go to school? ____________________

3 ______ you play football? ____________________

4 ______ you watch a film? ____________________

5 ______ you read an English book? ____________________

6 ______ you go to a carnival? ____________________

What about you? 3 Write.

Tomorrow, I'll ________________________________

____ .

Tomorrow, I won't ________________________________

____ .

1 Answer the questions.

1 What's the most famous holiday in your country?

____

2 Does it happen every year? ____________

3 How long does it last? ____________

4 How do people celebrate? ____________

5 Are there decorations in the streets? ____________

6 Do people eat special food? ____________

2 Cut out pictures from magazines.

3 Make a picture of people celebrating your most famous holiday.

LESSON 5 UNIT 12

1 **Circle eleven more words in the wordsquare. Write them in the correct boxes.**

Everyday items
1 poster

Animals: parts of the body
2 ____________

Food
3 ____________

Jewellery
4 ____________

At the farm
5 ____________

Containers
6 ____________

In the city
7 ____________

Chores
8 ____________

Countries
9 ____________

Nature
10 ____________

Jobs
11 ____________

At the carnival
12 ____________

p	o	s	t	e	r	l	k	e	e
i	o	b	u	i	l	d	e	r	g
p	n	p	r	d	m	k	l	m	y
b	e	a	k	c	f	l	a	b	p
c	c	x	e	e	a	a	m	o	t
l	k	r	y	r	w	u	p	t	p
c	l	o	w	n	y	n	p	t	d
c	a	c	t	u	s	d	o	l	w
q	c	r	d	h	o	r	s	e	q
y	e	p	p	c	k	y	t	y	u

2 **Complete. Use words from the wordsquare.**

1 I live in ____________.

2 My cousin is a ____________.

3 I love chicken but I don't like ____________.

4 She's wearing a beautiful ____________.

5 That bird has got a red ____________.

6 We always do the ____________ at the weekend.

3 Choose and write.

1. I'm visiting / I've visited ________ the USA three times.
2. played / going to play She's ________ tennis tomorrow.
3. rains / was raining It ________ at 2 o'clock yesterday.
4. won't watch / didn't watch They ________ TV last night.
5. will be / used to be I ________ rich, but now I'm poor.

4 Make the sentences negative.

1. My brother used to like cheese. My brother didn't use to like cheese.
2. We're going to stay at home tomorrow. ________
3. These dinosaurs had long necks. ________
4. I was listening to you. ________
5. We have to go shopping tomorrow. ________
6. She's cleaned her bedroom. ________
7. He could speak English last year. ________
8. We'll be late for school. ________

5 Order the words to make questions. Then write true answers.

1. tomorrow? / do / you / What / are / going / to

____

2. football / play / you / Did / yesterday?

____

3. shorter / teacher? / you / Are / your / than

____

4. in / tallest / Who's / the / the / student / class?

____

5. ever / Have / chess? / you / played

____

Phonics

1 Read.

Only clowns **w**ear **w**igs **wh**en it's **w**indy.

Only clowns **w**ash the **w**indows **w**ith **wh**ipped cream.

Only clowns have **wh**eels that are square.

Only clowns **w**ear **wh**ite shorts in the **w**inter.

2 Write *w* or *wh* to match the words in the story.

1 ____ ite
2 ____ eels
3 ____ ear
4 ____ ash
5 ____ indy
6 ____ en
7 ____ igs
8 ____ ith
9 ____ ipped
10 ____ inter

3 Look at the story and number the sentences.

1 Only clowns have wheels that are square. ☐
2 Only clowns wear white shorts in the winter. ☐
3 Only clowns wear wigs when it's windy. ☐
4 Only clowns wash windows with whipped cream. ☐

Try It!

LESSON 8 UNIT 12

What about you? **1 Complete the sentences using *I'll* or *I won't*.**

When I'm older ...

1 ________ be a vet.

2 ________ have a beard.

3 ________ have a dog.

4 ________ work in the city.

5 ________ work on a farm.

6 ________ study Japanese.

7 ________ go to India.

8 ________ swim every day.

9 ________ be a scientist.

10 ________ do the laundry.

11 ________ collect fossils.

12 ________ have a grandfather clock.

2 Find the opposites.

1 [h] could
2 [ ] better
3 [ ] tomorrow
4 [ ] can
5 [ ] take
6 [ ] clean
7 [ ] asked
8 [ ] herbivores
9 [ ] newer
10 [ ] thinner
11 [ ] the cheapest
12 [ ] the longest

a yesterday
b the shortest
c answered
d older
e carnivores
f give
g can't
h ~~couldn't~~
i the most expensive
j worse
k fatter
l dirty

The Challenge

1 Solve the puzzles. Then number the pictures and read.

1 ______________ juggler
2 ______________ dancer
3 ______________ fire-eater
4 ______________ clown
5 ______________ acrobat
6 ______________ carnival

The clown's eating candyfloss.

The dancer's dancing the samba.

The juggler's juggling balls.

The carnival happens at night.

The acrobat has a beard.

The fire-eaters are on the float.

2 Complete.

Things you could see at a carnival:	Things you could see at a birthday party:
1 ______________	1 ______________
2 ______________	2 ______________
3 ______________	3 ______________
4 ______________	4 ______________

3 Memory quiz. Answer the questions.

How much can you remember about Tara?

1 Who is Tara's Superhero?

____

2 What new toy would Tara like?

____

3 What's Tara's favourite festival?

____

4 What's Tara's favourite sea animal?

____

5 How many colas has Tara had?

____

6 What was Tara doing last night?

____

7 What would Tara like to be?

____

8 How many posters does Tara have?

____

I hope you enjoyed my quiz. Have a great holiday!

9 Where was Tara born?

____

10 Where did Tara go on her best holiday?

____

11 Where does Tara's mum work?

____

Wordlist

Unit 1

Everyday items
poster
laptop
chess set
camera
calendar
comb
briefcase
hairbrush
suitcase
watch
lamp
mirror
rug
bookcase

Phrases
Good luck!
So do I.
It's a secret!

Clocks
digital clock
sundial
candle clock
grandfather clock

Other
costume
touch
join
barbecue
planet
superhero
year
leaving
heavy
spell

Unit 2

Animal body parts
beak
wing
neck
horns
spikes
scales
back
back legs

Dinosaurs
dinosaur
pterosaur
diplodocus
tyrannosaurus rex
triceratops
stegosaurus
plesiosaurus
ichthyosaurus
pterodactyl
fossil/s

Other
herbivores
carnivores
reptiles
enormous
millions
ago
around
attendant
popcorn
really
the front
cave
buffalo
slave
wherever
rattlesnake
beneath
passing
humans
groups
volleyball
nest
money
storm
cliff
crocodile
first
important
discovery/ies
complete
sharp
classmates
window
robbers
coin
bright
silver

Verbs
ask/asked
shout/shouted
answer/answered
press/pressed
live/lived
change/changed
jump/jumped
turned
notice/noticed
attack
bought
follow
heard
met
slept
laid
brought
collect
wanted
born
called

helped
found
became
climbed
stole
thinks
flies
threw
danced
ate
drank
left

Phrases
Look out!
That's impossible.
They lived millions of years ago.
for example ...

Unit 3

The Feast
potatoes
bread rolls
butter
meat
soup
salad
green beans
apple pie
turkey
meal
bowl/s
plate/s
vegetables
festival

Verbs
could/couldn't
smell
looked
celebrate
build
taught
invited
standing up
disappeared
carries

Other
middle
delicious
century
strangers
secretly
bricks
Ramadan
Muslim
fasting
sohour
iftar
lanterns
fanous
genius
languages
university
chess
Japanese
English
Chinese
(the) bottom
(a) well
(the) top
news reporter

Phrases
Yes, of course.
Don't you know?
Help yourself!
Could you help (me) please?

Unit 4

Jewellery and accessories
boots
beard
jacket
glasses
earrings
necklace
ring
bracelet

Verbs
used to
arriving
skipping
thumping
wear

Other
daughter
monster
hollow
misty
fog
heart/s
conservatory
loud
nobody
too
radio
singer
fans
expensive
harbour
nothing
swimmer

Phrases
I didn't use it.
I used to have one.
I haven't got one now.
Let's get out of here!
What's the matter?
We're sinking!
I don't think so.
Ouch!

Wordlist

That hurts!
You took a long time!

Unit 5

At the farm

sheep
cows
goats
cock
hen
hedge
barn
hay
horse
farm
gate
grass
cattle
field
tractor
ducks
farmhouse

Verbs

trying
making
hiding
standing
shining
sleeping
taking care
attacking
lie/lying
working
called
rang
asked
answered
explain
take back
escaped
smiles

Other

dream
(the) past
village
busy
wolf
villagers
e-mails
telephone
robbery
library
guests
hot chocolate
television room
notebook
noise
safari park

Phrases

There you are!
Don't you remember?
Everything changed again.
Come quickly!
I'm going to take it back.
What were you doing ...?
Calm down!

Unit 6

Containers and shops

box
tin
bottle
tube
pack
bag
bar
jar
supermarket
candles
honey
flour
paint
crayons
toothpaste
glue
soap
basket
cereal
chillies
orange juice

Phrases

You're right.
It isn't my fault.
It sells all kinds of things.
Tara is taller than Todd.
You have flour all over you!
Can't you be more careful?
It's time to disappear.
Anything else?
Here you are.
How much is that?
Show us!
I knew it!
It's too small/big ...
Which (line) is (longer)?

Comparative adjectives

smaller
higher
shorter
more careful
bigger
older
younger
taller
larger
fatter
thinner
heavier
lighter
braver
faster

cleverer
hotter
longer
better
newer
slower
more comfortable
more expensive
cheaper
more exciting
stronger
worse
cleaner
dirtier

Other
kinds
a lot of
measure
carpet
train
picks up
tell

Unit 7

City streets
pavement
rubbish bin
post box
lamp post
bus stop
newsagent
restaurant
zebra crossing
street
advertisement
cities
capital
shopping centre
lorry
bed shop

Superlative adjectives
busiest
cheapest
best
worst
nicest
friendliest
smallest
largest
tallest
biggest
most expensive
most exciting
dirtiest
coldest
hottest
wettest
sunniest

Other
opposite
probably
date
(the) future
flat
Tokyo
Japan
Mexico City
Beijing
Fairbanks
USA
temperature
degrees
Celsius
Australia
enough
icy
sounds
trouble
mattress

Phrases
Great!
At last.
I have no idea.
It's too heavy.
I'm not strong enough.
That sounds like trouble!
That lorry is out of control!
Nobody could understand!

Unit 8

Chores
feed the dog/cat
water the plants
do the washing-up
do the laundry
make the bed
sweep the floor
clean the windows
do the ironing
go fishing
collect water
(help with the) housework
clean
take out the rubbish
do my homework

Other
department store
rubbish
way
Amazon rain forest
Brazil
share
well
twins
Seoul
South Korea
grandmother
pairs
inside

Wordlist

hard
leave
seconds
messy
minutes

Games

counters
dice
turns
move
square
roll
go back
start
miss
count
forward

Phrases

I want one!
We have to stop it!
Pick it up!
We have to find a different way!
every day
See you later!

Unit 9

Countries and cities

Mexico
India
Egypt
Hollywood
Seoul
Sydney
Rio de Janeiro
Mumbai
London
Acapulco
Cairo
Peru
Ecuador
Florida
Caribbean
Australia
Bondi Beach
Aborigines
outback
Great Barrier Reef
Uluru
Northern Territory
states

Other

magazines
virtual reality tour
hill
salsa band
one-man band
sparkling
hurricane
island
deep breath
direction

Verbs

noticed
entered
followed
travelled
repaired
brushed
combed
worried
destroyed
reached
blows
changes

Phrases

What are we waiting for?
Let's follow him!
Can I help you?
Have they ...?
Yes, they have. / No, they haven't.
They have/n't (played) (football).
We're late!

Unit 10

Nature

stream
palm tree
waterfall
sand
coconuts
cactus
leaf/leaves
animals
sand
oxygen
rain
snow
land
sea

Verbs

seen
swum
ridden
eaten
slept
lost
found
gone
been
met
made
given
had
cut down
fallen down
blocking

Other
thirsty
still
Costa Rica
Canada
Indonesia
useful
things
originally
Spanish
geography

Phrases
I don't get it.
At last!
Have you ever ...?

Unit 11

Jobs
scientist
magician
house painter
builder
vet
window cleaner
photographer
teacher

Phrases
Good idea!
Oh dear!
Let's try it!
That's better!
What's that smell?

Inventions
CDs
cassettes
DVDs
cinemas
camera
vacuum cleaner
tin opener
sewing machine
electric light

Verbs
throws
explodes
holds
ties
finds
starts
thinks
flies
guesses
knits
cleans
hides
takes
opens
plays
wears

Other
magic spell
pipes
helmet
robot
button
rocket
through
space
outside
knot
amazed
truth

Unit 12

Parades and carnivals
juggler
acrobats
clowns
fire-eater
dancers
storytellers
hot dogs
float
candyfloss
parties
costumes
dance
streets
musicians
festival

Phrases
It's a long story.
What's going on?
What's wrong?
That's great!
I promise.
Nothing's wrong.

Verbs
wearing
eating
talking
happening

Other
happier
sunshine
clarinet
guests
dreaming
voice
completely
boring
helmet
delicious

Macmillan Education
Between Towns Road, Oxford OX4 3PP
A division of Macmillan Publishers Limited
Companies and representatives throughout the world

ISBN 978-1-4050-5949-7

First published 2004

Designed by MKR Design Limited
Page make-up by Zed

Illustrated by:
Dawn Adlam/Creative Design: (pages 2, 8, 10, 19, 20,22, 29, 30, 37, 39, 40, 45, 52, 55, 57, 58, 69, 78, 79, 97, 99, 102, 103, 105, 106, 108, 110, 112).
Beehive (pages 25, 26, 43, 49, 63, 92)
Art Explosion/Nova Development: (pages 5, 15, 35, 45, 55, 65, 75, 85, 95, 105, 115).
Ken Bowser: (page 1).
Dan Crisp: (pages 3, 4, 7, 8, 10, 11, 14, 16, 20, 21, 23, 28, 30, 31, 33, 36, 40, 41, 44, 48, 50, 51, 53, 57, 60, 61, 67, 70, 71, 73, 77, 80, 81, 90, 91, 96, 100, 101, 106, 110, 111, 120, 121).
Robin Edmonds: (pages 5, 6, 9, 11, 15, 17, 18, 23, 25, 26, 33, 34, 35, 36, 38, 42, 43, 47, 49, 49, 50, 54, 59, 60, 62, 63, 65, 66, 72, 75, 76, 82, 83, 85, 86, 87, 89, 90, 91, 92, 95, 96, 109, 116, 119, 120).
Alison Kelt: (page 115).
Steve Molloy: (pages 3, 4, 7, 8, 10, 11, 14, 16, 20, 21, 23, 28, 30, 31, 33, 36, 40, 41, 44, 48, 50, 51, 53, 57, 60, 61, 67, 70, 71, 73, 77, 80, 81, 90, 91, 96, 100, 101, 106, 110, 111, 120, 121).
Cover design by Linda Reed & Associates
Cover illustration by Steve Molloy, Just for Laffs

Printed and bound in Egypt by Sahara Printing Company

2013 2012 2011 2010
10 9 8 7